TO PHIL CAMP

Thanks for your interest
in Richard Lapointe.

Steve Greenspan

CONVICTING THE INNOCENT

CONVICTING THE INNOCENT

The Story of a Murder,
a False Confession,
and the Struggle to Free
a "Wrong Man"

Edited by DONALD S. CONNERY

 **BROOKLINE BOOKS**

ISBN 1-57129-021-4

Cover art and design by Jane Heft, Morra Design, Bristol, CT.
Book design and typography by Erica Schultz.
Printed in the USA by Bradford & Bigelow, Danvers, MA.

Library of Congress Cataloging-In-Publication Data
Convicting the innocent : the story of a murder, a false confession,
    and the struggle to free a "wrong man" / edited by Donald S.
    Connery.
        220 p.   cm.
        Includes index.
        ISBN 1-57129-021-4 (pbk.)
        1. Lapointe, Richard, 1946-   . 2. Homicide–Connecticut–
    Manchester–Case studies.   3. Mentally handicapped–Civil rights–
    Connecticut–Manchester–Case studies.   4. Mentally handicapped and
    crime–Connecticut–Manchester–Case studies.   5. Prisoners–Civil
    rights–Connecticut–Manchester–Case studies.   6. False
    imprisonment–Connecticut–Manchester–Case studies.   7. Criminal
    justice, Administration of–Connecticut–Manchester–Case studies.
    I. Connery, Donald S.
    HV6534.M26C66   1996
    364.1'523'097462–dc20   95-49419
                                                                          CIP

BROOKLINE BOOKS

P.O. Box 1047, Cambridge, Massachusetts 02238

Contents

PART III
REPORTS OF A QUEST FOR JUSTICE

PART IV
FREEDOM FOR JOHNNY LEE WILSON AND
ROLANDO CRUZ;
THE FIGHT FOR RICHARD LAPOINTE GOES ON

Preface and Acknowledgments

Donald S. Connery

Be warned:

If you read this book you will never think about the criminal justice system in the same way again.

You will be appalled — perhaps horrified — by the dirtiest secret in the darkest corner of law enforcement.

But you may also be inspired by the actions taken by average citizens who believe that being strong for justice is no less important than being tough on crime.

Though this book takes a sweeping, nationwide look at the enduring scandal of "wrong-man" convictions, its design is to illuminate the whole by focusing intensely on a single sequence of events: a vicious murder, the selection of an exceptionally vulnerable innocent man as a convenient way to close an embarrassing case, and the crusade of the people who would not let the deed go unnoticed.

It is a tale told through the different perspectives of scholars, attorneys, authors, investigative journalists, advocates for the mentally disabled, specialists on the human mind, and the men and women of conscience who first raised the alarm.

Consider it, if you will, the anatomy of an injustice.

Or a national disgrace: the American equivalent of "the disappeared" in less humane societies who are dispatched to oblivion.

Is this an exaggeration? Read the book.

See it as a rare opportunity to understand how it is possible today, in the nation that was meant to be the opposite of an inquisitorial society, for a blameless person to be falsely accused, wrongfully convicted, and given life behind bars or a seat on Death Row — not on evidence, not for good reasons, but because of words torn from his own mouth.

Then realize that this one case is just the tip of the iceberg. Observe through the dozens of other stories described or mentioned in these pages that this is no dirty *little* secret. It is a larger calamity and a larger conspiracy of silence than anyone knows; certainly larger than the conservative accounting given here by several of the country's leading historians of the phenomenon.

At issue is the whole business of "solving" crimes with uncorroborated confessions. At issue, too, is the way the system pretends that miscarriages of justice occur only rarely and never intentionally.

Particularly egregious are the approved police methods that can *create* guilt (while giving criminals a free pass) by compelling poor, powerless, naive, ill-educated, mentally impaired or simply exhausted and befuddled subjects to admit to crimes they did not commit. Suspects are then turned over to prosecutors who, too often, are more interested in winning than in being sure that justice is done.

It happens.

It happens over and over again.

It happens because most cops, prosecutors and judges choose to believe that no sane person, short of physical torture, can be induced to confess to a crime if innocent.

Never mind the power of suggestion, techniques of persuasion and intimidation, and all knowledge about the ability of the strong to crush the weak.

The fiction that denies false confessions was thoroughly dissected one fine day in mid-September 1995 by experts from seven states during a six-hour public forum in a major auditorium in Hartford, Connecticut. The event was organized by a group of citizens working to free the central character of this book: a brain-damaged menial laborer named Richard Lapointe, now in his seventh year in prison.

They were people who were dissatisfied with the slow-working appeal process that may or may not overturn Lapointe's conviction some future day. To them, it had been an act of immorality for the state to so recklessly destroy a man and his family. And now it seemed immoral for the state, knowing the plain facts of his innocence, to keep him incarcerated instead of moving heaven and earth to set him free.

Three years earlier, when the citizens first came together to find a way to help, they could not have imagined that persistence in the face of endless frustrations would lead in time to a historic gathering of national authorities on wrongful convictions.

What made the event unprecedented was the clear intention of the organizers to take a giant step beyond the rescue of one man. Their ambition was to make the forum the beginning of a process that would bring about certain critical reforms in the American justice system: the need to record interrogations, the need to assist mentally disabled suspects, recompense for persons erroneously imprisoned, and a greater professional disdain for cases built on the extraction of so-called admissions.

The success of this forum gave them a tool to do this work: the book you are about to read. It is a compilation of the proceedings sandwiched between the best of the early and the most recent press accounts of the Lapointe case. In some instances, the addresses and dialogue have been condensed or edited for clarity and accuracy.

All royalties, apart from funds necessary to win Lapointe's freedom, will go to long-term efforts to create a national awareness of the law's indifference to false confessions and of the exploitation of accused persons who are too mentally limited to understand their rights.

Who are these people who love justice so much?

To acknowledge all who have contributed in great or small ways to this endeavor would make a list too long and too likely to be incomplete. And how exactly do you measure the value of a law professor's advice, a volunteer's willingness to address fund-raising letters, or the regular prison visits of those who keep a man's hopes alive?

What does seem sensible is to first tell of the two public defenders who put heart and soul into the case for Lapointe's innocence, Pat Culligan and Chris Cosgrove, and the two dedicated defense attorneys who are working now without charge for his freedom: John Williams and Norman Pattis.

Then to honor two great men of letters for their willingness to speak for justice: Arthur Miller and William Styron.

And finally to set down the names of those individuals who have been particularly unflagging over the years in the Lapointe cause, or whose labors have been vital to the making of the *Convicting the Inno-*

cent forum and this book.

They are: Dot Amundsen, Cynthia Bania, Norman Bania, Thelma Bauer, Pat Beeman, John Castle, Margene Castle, Leslie Connery, Marge Cunningham, Peg Dignoti, George Ducharme, Richard Furman, Ron Gould, Stephen Greenspan, Irving Hargrave, Rosemarie Hargrave, Angela Hauptman, Kevin Hinchey, Roger Kent, Clair Langton, Mary-Ann Langton, Andy Lefebvre, Florence Lefebvre, Diane Lewis, Michelle Livingston, Georgiana Nadeau, Terri Nadeau, John Nolte, Tracey O'Brien, Robert Perske, Rachel Singer, Millie Strickland, Eleanor Sweeney, and Richard Wilson.

Introduction

William Styron

In a nation that has become increasingly rancorous about the soft treatment of criminals, and is willing, in the name of punishment, to tolerate the most flagrant errors of its criminal justice system, the idea of casting Richard Lapointe as a victim may appear a trifle sentimental. Retribution (often blind) is the current watchword, and those clamoring for more rigorous law and order have little patience with even the most incapacitated losers. Grim examples abound. In 1985, the Reverend Joe Ingle, a prominent anti-death penalty advocate, visited Morris Mason an hour before his electrocution for murder at the Virginia State Penitentiary in Richmond. Mason, a 32-year-old black man with an IQ of 66, was so uncomprehending of his fate that he solemnly asked Ingle to tell another Death Row prisoner that he would be back soon to play basketball with him.

Richard Lapointe's intelligence is not quite so deficient as that of Morris Mason, but he is badly brain-damaged; the 50-year-old dishwasher, presently serving a life sentence for rape and homicide in a Connecticut prison, is also really unable to comprehend his plight, confused enough about what has happened to him to telephone a supporter from time to time and ask, "When am I going to get out?" Lapointe has as strong a claim to victimhood as any mentally handicapped person could possibly present, having suffered not only the justice system's obvious malfeasance, but also its amnesia. For in fact only slightly more than two decades ago, also in Connecticut, there was enacted another miscarriage of justice — one celebrated to such a degree that one can only wonder how Lapointe, whose case in important respects resembles the earlier one, could have been submitted to such ruinous mistreatment.

On a September night in 1973, an 18-year-old boy, Peter Reilly, returned to his home in the small community of Falls Village, a part of the town of Canaan, and discovered the naked and mutilated body of his mother, Barbara Gibbons. After the arrival of the ambulance, which he summoned himself, Peter was taken into custody by the state police, who began a marathon interrogation and were delighted when he volunteered to take a so-called lie detector test. At this point, Peter's confession became the crucial factor in his trial and conviction for manslaughter. Because Richard Lapointe's own conviction hung almost entirely upon a confession extracted under coercive circumstances, I'd like to quote from my own observations on this aspect of the Reilly case, which I set down in my introduction to Joan Barthel's narrative account, *A Death in Canaan.*

Like nearly all the law-enforcement officers in the drama, Sergeant [Timothy] Kelly is "nice;" it is as hard to conceive of him with a truncheon or blackjack as with a volume of Proust. Plainly, neither Kelly nor his colleague Lieutenant [James] Shay, who was actually responsible for Peter's confession, are vicious men; they are merely undiscerningly obedient, devoid of that flexibility of mind we call imagination, and they both have a passionate faith in the machine. Kelly, especially, is an unquestioning votary. "We go strictly by the charts," he tells an exhausted boy. "And the charts say you hurt your mother last night."

In a society where everything sooner or later breaks down, where cars fall apart and ovens explode and vacuum cleaners expire through planned obsolescence, there is something awesome about the sergeant's pious belief in the infallibility of his polygraph. And so at a point in his ordeal, Peter, tired and confused, only hours removed from the trauma of witnessing his mother's mutilated body, asks, "Have you ever been proven totally wrong? A person, just from nervousness, responds that way?" Kelly replies, "No, the polygraph can never be wrong. It's the person interpreting it who could be wrong. But I haven't made that mistake in twelve years, in the thousands of people who sat here, Pete." Such mighty

faith and assurance would have alone been enough to deci-
sively wipe out a young man at the end of his tether. Add to
this faith the presumed assumption of guilt on the part of
the sergeant, and the tendentious nature of his questioning,
and it's no wonder that a numb and bedraggled Peter was a
setup for Lieutenant Shay, whose manner of extracting a
confession from this troubled boy must be deemed a triumph of benevolent intimidation.

After his conviction, Peter Reilly began serving time in prison,
but there were so many people convinced of his innocence — virtually
all of the physical evidence connected with the crime was unpersuasive;
time elements were out of kilter; but most importantly, there was
simply no motivation for a kid of Peter's worthy character — that
public pressure, media revelations, and new evidence produced by a
new defense team caused the judge who had presided over the trial to
grant a new one. Before the second trial could begin, however, the
state's attorney dropped dead on a golf course. His young successor
was astonished to find hidden in the case files crucial statements by
credible eyewitnesses who had seen Peter in his car five miles from the
murder scene at the precise time that he was said to be home attacking his mother. Peter went free. He has been a valuable member of the
community ever since.

It is plain that of the various factors that militated against this
innocent young man, and that came close to blighting his life with
soul-crippling prison time, the most decisive and sinister was his confession, extracted with repellent benignity.

Richard Lapointe's life sentence for murder also hinges upon a
confession, a secret confession whose falseness appears more glaringly
apparent as the story of this mild-mannered man's life and background
— and also his alleged crime — unfolds.

On March 8, 1987, in the town of Manchester, Bernice Martin,
who was the 88-year-old grandmother of Lapointe's wife, was raped
and murdered. Over two years later, frustrated by their inability to
find the murderer, the police took Lapointe, who had no history of
violence, into custody and submitted him to a grilling that lasted
more than nine hours. During this period he signed three confessions. It would seem important at this point to touch upon the na-

ture of the man, and of the man's mind, exposed to such relentless non-stop interrogation. Lapointe was born with part of his brain, the cerebellum, missing that portion of tissue which governs not only bodily coordination (he is physically awkward) but cognition of a higher order. He has undergone five operations to correct the underlying pathology. Although that vastly inaccurate barometer of intelligence, the IQ test, has been, in Lapointe's case, established at the "low average" level of 92 — thereby permitting the accusation that his retardation is not so great as to have let him confess to a crime he didn't commit — his impairment is nonetheless grievous enough to have made him a pushover for persistent inquisitors. The syndrome that afflicts him, known as Dandy-Walker, has been widely observed and well documented; it has been shown to produce a deficit in social intelligence, with often predictable characteristics. In an essay included in the present volume, Stephen Greenspan, a developmental psychologist who has studied this particular disability, and who has closely examined Lapointe as well, convincingly demonstrates his subject's pathetic vulnerability in the face of a procedure aimed at extracting, at any cost, an admission of guilt. At any rate, Lapointe signed the three confessions, which during the trial were shown, through forensic evidence, to contain such inconsistencies and contradictions as to make one conclusion inescapable. He said what the police wanted him to say.

There is an interesting distinction between Lapointe's case and that of Peter Reilly. Whatever the appalling deficiencies of Peter's interrogation, it was at least recorded on tape. Indeed, it might be said that one of the factors leading to Peter Reilly's eventual vindication was the audiotape made during his ruthless grilling; it clearly revealed the browbeating methods of coercion used upon an exhausted boy, and helped many people make up their minds about the police and their subtle brutality. But Lapointe was denied even this rudimentary protection, and such a failure might provide a warning for the future. Recording not merely the voices but all aspects of the interrogation by videotape should be made mandatory for the benefit of everyone concerned, including the police. Likewise, there is a need to safeguard the rights of anyone accused of a crime, but especially the mentally handicapped, by the presence of a neutral observer at the time of questioning.

But nothing seems to have been learned from the Reilly affair over the years, in a pocket-sized state where the two crimes, both widely publicized, occurred scarcely forty miles apart. In any case, what Lapointe actually said during that nine-hour ordeal was, in the end, irrelevant. It only matters that this small man of meager wit incriminated himself. Confessions, no matter how intrinsically inauthentic they may be, tend to have an effect on juries like Holy Writ, and Lapointe's confession lost him his freedom, already so circumscribed by a mind limited in dreams and possibilities. He has now been locked up for six and a half years.

Is there any hope for Richard Lapointe? Even the most unsophisticated newspaper reader is aware that, in criminal cases where justice has been miscarried, authorities will fight furiously to avoid any admission of their own mistakes. This gives an illusion of the law's universal rectitude. It was demonstrated in the Peter Reilly affair, when, one year after all charges were dropped against Peter, the state police doggedly tried (without success) to have the young man put on trial again. Fear of loss of face is often the overriding factor, and the authorities in the case of Richard Lapointe seem determined to protect themselves from the obvious appearance of being not prosecutors, but persecutors, by rejecting any suggestion of error, much less delinquency.

There have been recent developments, however, that give rise to the hope that our unconscionable treatment of mentally handicapped defendants is becoming a matter of public and official consciousness. In late September 1995, there walked out of the gates of the Missouri Correctional Center a retarded 30-year-old inmate, Johnny Lee Wilson, who was freed after having served ten years of a life sentence without parole for a murder of which he was innocent. As in the case of Richard Lapointe, the victim was an elderly woman, and the accused made a false confession after a long and harrowing interrogation. An official review revealed that the defendant had given his questioners those answers he felt would "get him out of trouble."

"We have locked up an innocent retarded man who is not guilty."

These words, chillingly freighted with an awareness of the law's fallibility — and also of the ever-present possibility of the law's malfeasance — were spoken by the governor of Missouri. In the matter of Richard Lapointe, while it is true that Connecticut's chief executive does not have the same pardoning power, it is clearly imperative that words just as strong and decent be spoken by the most powerful figures of the place that calls itself "The Constitution State."

PART I

REPORTS OF A WRONGFUL CONVICTION

The Richard Lapointe Case Chronology

1987 MARCH 8: Bernice Martin, 88, of Manchester, Connecticut, is raped, stabbed 11 times and strangled. She is left inside to die as her apartment in a senior citizens complex is set on fire.

1987-1988 Manchester police, led by Detective Michael Ludlow, work from a list of 38 suspects but fail to solve the crime.

1989 JUNE: Detective Paul Lombardo, assigned to review the investigation, focuses on Richard Lapointe, 43, husband of the victim's granddaughter, Karen. Lapointe had been interviewed earlier because, in response to a call from a worried relative, he had gone to the apartment and discovered the fire.

JULY 4: On this Independence Day, Lapointe, asked to help the police with their inquiries, is driven to headquarters in mid-afternoon. He is read his Miranda rights and then accused of murder.

For the next nine and a half hours he is interrogated without legal counsel, first by Lombardo, then by detective Michael Morrissey, and finally by Captain Joseph Brooks.

No tape or other record of the questioning is made, or so the police say, but a simultaneous two-hour interview at home with Karen Lapointe is secretly taped by detective Morrissey, with the assistance of his brother — a fact revealed accidentally, years later, just before Lapointe's trial.

Despite repeated denials of any involvement in the killing, Lapointe signs three "confessions," as set down by the detectives. After midnight, he is told he is free to go. Waiting family members drive him home to his wife and 10-year-old son after midnight.

JULY 5: After a few hours sleep, Lapointe, believing he is no longer a suspect, goes to work as usual to his dishwashing job. In the evening, he is arrested at home on the basis of an affidavit written by Lombardo and an arrest warrant signed by Superior Court Judge Raymond R. Norko. Unable to post $500,000 bond, he is jailed — and has remained behind bars ever since.

AUGUST 23 & 25: Following a preliminary hearing in Hartford Superior Court, Judge Harry Hammer finds there is sufficient evidence to try Lapointe for the murder of Bernice Martin.

MID-1989 TO 1991   Lapointe, unable to afford an attorney, waits two and a half years in several prisons for his day in court.

1991   DECEMBER 16: Hearing on Lapointe's motion to suppress the confession begins in Hartford Superior Court before Judge David M. Barry. Lapointe is represented by public defenders Patrick Culligan and Christopher Cosgrove. The prosecutors are Rosita Creamer and John Malone, working under the direction of State's Attorney John M. Bailey.

1992   FEBRUARY 18: Suppression hearing concludes.

MARCH 6: Judge Barry refuses to suppress the confession.

MAY 6: Trial begins after weeks of jury selection. Creamer is the lead prosecutor, now assisted by Dennis O'Connor.

JUNE 30: Jury finds Lapointe guilty of capital felony murder and eight related charges.

JULY 29: The state seeks the death penalty but, following a long hearing, the jury decides against capital punishment for Lapointe.

SEPTEMBER 6: Judge Barry sentences Lapointe to life imprisonment without the possibility of parole, plus 60 years.

Soon afterward, citizens who had attended the trial, including advocates for persons with mental impairments, begin meeting regularly as The Friends of Richard Lapointe. In their view, a miscarriage of justice has occurred. They say his conviction was based not on evidence but on a false confession elicited from an easily intimidated man with significant brain damage who could not understand his rights.

1993 FEBRUARY 21: *The Hartford Courant*'s Sunday magazine, *Northeast*, publishes "Reasonable Doubt," a long investigative report of the Martin slaying and Lapointe's prosecution by law-trained columnist Tom Condon. He concludes that Lapointe is innocent.

During the remainder of the year, The Friends of Richard Lapointe attempt to raise public and media awareness about the case but with little success. They are frustrated by the length of time required for typing the transcripts of court proceedings that are necessary for preparation of the appeal brief to the Connecticut Supreme Court.

1994 MID-YEAR: Transcripts are finally available. Attorney John R. Williams agrees to represent Lapointe without charge for the appeal. The citizens group gains new members and professional assistance as Lapointe's story wins greater press attention. Playwright Arthur Miller, a key figure in correcting the famous Peter Reilly wrongful conviction in the 1970s, speaks of the Lapointe case as another apparent miscarriage of justice in an address at the Connecticut Bar Association's annual dinner.

NOVEMBER 29: A Connecticut Public Television documentary, *A Passion for Justice,* centers on the Lapointe case in a report on writer/advocate Robert Perske and his work with persons with mental retardation who encounter the justice system.

1995 JANUARY 9-13: The *Journal Inquirer* of Manchester publishes a detailed analysis by staff writer Alex Wood that exposes the police lies and deceits that led to Lapointe's arrest and prosecution.

FEBRUARY 27: Filing of Lapointe's appeal brief by attorneys John Williams and Norman Pattis to the Connecticut Supreme Court. It seeks new law requiring recording of interrogations that produce confessions.

The four issues presented: "1. Whether the due process clause of the Connecticut Supreme Court requires electronic taping of confessions and advisement of *Miranda* rights. 2. Whether the trial court clearly erred in concluding that the defendant was not in custody during his second and third confessions. 3. Whether the trial court erred in ruling that Mr. Lapointe knowingly and intelligently waived his right to counsel. 4. Whether the trial court erred in denying Mr. Lapointe the right to confront one of the state's witnesses against him."

SEPTEMBER 4: Inclusion International (International League of Societies for Persons with Mental Handicap), representing 169 organizations in 105 countries, issues a "Statement on Behalf of Richard Lapointe" decrying his wrongful conviction and calling on "the responsible authorities" to set him free speedily.

SEPTEMBER 7: At a Hartford Club press conference, spokesmen for The Friends of Richard Lapointe tell of futile efforts for more than a year to persuade Chief State's Attorney John M. Bailey to re-examine the Lapointe case. They call for his resignation.

SEPTEMBER 16: An unprecedented six-hour public forum on "Convicting the Innocent," with experts from six states as well as Connecticut, takes place in the Aetna auditorium, Hartford, under the sponsorship of The Friends of Richard Lapointe and Arc/CT (formerly The Association for Retarded Citizens of Connecticut).

NOVEMBER 17: Filing at the Connecticut Supreme Court of the state's response to the defense appeal brief of February 27. While acknowledging that "there may be some benefits to be gained by recording confessions taken in a custodial situation," the state declares that "Connecticut's history demonstrates that there was never a concern for the recording of confessions" and that Lapointe's constitutional rights were not violated.

EVENTS TO COME: 1) Filing of the defense reply to the state's brief; 2) oral arguments before the court in early 1996; 3) the court's decision in mid-1996 responding to the appeal that Lapointe's conviction be vacated "and this matter remanded for a new trial."

REASONABLE DOUBT

Richard Lapointe, Prisoner Number 184163,
Is Inarticulate and Bumbling.
But Is He Really a *Murderer*?
Tom Condon *Doesn't* Think So.

By TOM CONDON

Fourth of July, 1989, midafternoon, and Richard Lapointe was going to have a picnic with his wife and son. The phone rang. It was the Manchester police. Could he come down to the station for a little chat? He'd be home in time for the holiday cookout.

Well, OK, he said. He didn't drive, so a detective came out to pick him up. Lapointe wondered if the officers wanted to talk to him, again, about the unsolved rape and murder of his wife's 88-year-old grandmother, Bernice Martin, more than two years earlier.

Their plan was actually a little more ambitious. Police hoped to make Lapointe confess to the crime.

To that end, an elaborate ruse had been planned. Two rooms in the station were festooned with props — pictures, charts, lists, and diagrams — that portrayed Lapointe as the killer. A chart said his fingerprints were found on a knife used in the crime. Another linked him to the crime through DNA testing. There was a list of detectives who were on the "Bernice Martin Homicide Task Force."

None of this was true. A suspect who carefully read the "squad assignments" on the task force list might have detected the hokum when he came across the team of "Friday and Gannon," the detectives in the later episodes of TV's *Dragnet*. Regardless, most people in Lapointe's situation would have realized they were in plenty of trouble.

But Lapointe, a homely, mentally handicapped man with no history of violence, hadn't a clue. He listened as a sergeant quickly read him his rights, then scribbled his name on a waiver form and went upstairs with a detective. Over the next nine hours, he gave police three statements admitting guilt in the rape and murder. Then they let him go home, and arrested him the next day.

He was convicted of the crime almost three years later in Superior Court

Richard Lapointe in prison.

on June 30, 1992. Although prosecutors fought to have him executed, he was sentenced to life in prison without chance of parole.

Police, jurors and prosecutors say they got the right man. But dozens of others — people who know Lapointe, advocates for handicapped persons, lawyers who followed the trial — find the case deeply troubling.

"As for protection of individual rights, it was the system at its worst. It was a bad case all around," said Hartford defense lawyer William Gerace, who followed the case. That was my reaction as well.

After attending parts of the trial, reviewing thousands of pages of transcripts, and speaking with more than two dozen people who were either involved in the trial or who know Lapointe, I have two problems with the case:

Lapointe didn't get a fair shake. Some believe criminal defendants are coddled and given too many rights and safeguards. Lapointe, who needed them if anyone does, got none. He had no lawyer, his statements weren't taped and his family wasn't allowed to call or visit during the nine-hour interrogation. Police subjected him to lies, tricks and intimidation to obtain his confession.

Also, I don't think Lapointe did it.

MR. MAGOO

Richard Lapointe, now 47, was born in Hartford and raised in Hartford's Charter Oak Terrace housing project. As a child he showed very little promise. He was, and is, short, chubby, weak, and awkward. He wears thick glasses and a hearing aid. He has a head too large for his body, a pointy chin, poor balance and a slow walk that is several degrees off plumb.

He was slow in school as well. Some kids picked on him and called him "Mister Magoo." The unfairness of this made one gang of kids take Richard under its wing. One of those kids was Jack Jenkins.

"He was the type of kid who, because of his physical stature and appearance, gets picked on. He couldn't fight back. He was the classic 90-pound weakling, so the group I hung out with looked after him," Jenkins said.

In one of life's little ironies, Jenkins had become deputy warden of the Bridgeport jail, where Lapointe was taken after being picked on in the Hartford jail. Jenkins recognized his walk as they brought him in and called out, "Magoo?" Then Jenkins did what he'd done three decades before: He looked out for Mister Magoo.

As a child, Lapointe had remained cheerful despite the ridicule. This was a point of pride; he told a psychologist years later that he felt bigger than the kids who taunted him when he smiled and walked away. He still tries to be accepted as the class clown by telling little jokes, the same jokes over and over, to make people like him.

It wasn't until he was 15 years old that doctors discovered why Lapointe was an inert student. He had Dandy-Walker Syndrome, a rare hereditary condition now treated at birth, in which a cyst in the lower back of the brain cavity causes parts of the brain to develop abnormally. The cyst often alters the flow of cerebral spinal fluid, causing hydrocephalus, a buildup of fluid that can damage a number of brain functions, such as coordination, speech, memory and abstract thinking.

Lapointe had the first of five brain operations at 15. Doctors put in a shunt, or tube, to draw the fluid out of the cranial cavity.

After his first operation, he tried to return to school. He'd stayed back three times in the first eight grades, then entered Hartford Public High School as a 17-year-old freshman. He didn't make it through the year. He said the school board suggested he drop out, because he was only taking up a seat.

Shortly thereafter, at 21, Lapointe was picked up for indecent exposure and intoxication. In a recent interview in Somers prison, he said he was walking home from a party with a rip in the crotch of his pants. He received a 10-day suspended sentence. It was his only trouble with the law until his arrest in the Martin case.

After he left school, he settled into life as a dishwasher in a variety of Hartford restaurants. In the mid-1970s he met Karen Martin, a young woman who had a mild case of cerebral palsy and had only partial use of one arm. They married, and in 1979 had a bright and handsome son, Sean. The delivery was difficult for Karen, so Richard had a vasectomy shortly thereafter.

They lived on Richard's dishwashing salary and occasional help from Karen's family. They were so poor at times that when Sean got older Richard would sometimes lower him into Salvation Army bins to grab clothes. Though they were poor, they ate out a good deal because their disabilities made cooking difficult. Waitresses who worked with Richard often gave him the "bombs," the food orders made incorrectly or sent back by customers. Yet the Lapointes struggled to lead a normal life, and somehow got by.

They settled in Manchester in the early '80s, near some of his wife's relatives. Their favorite was Karen's grandmother, Bernice Martin, whom they called "Nana" or "Mother." Mrs. Martin, a former teacher and Sears saleswoman, was by all accounts an inspirational woman with myriad interests; she organized bingo games and Bible readings for her friends, wrote poems, loved sports, and baked cookies for the volunteer firemen.

She lived in a housing complex for the elderly, Mayfair Gardens, a collection of one-story, wood-and-brick shoeboxes a couple of blocks from the Lapointe home in the north end of town. Richard and Karen settled into a routine that included regular visits to Mrs. Martin's house on Sundays. The Lapointes, devout Catholics, would attend Mass at St. Bridget's Church, have brunch at My Brother's Place, a restaurant on North Main Street, then cross the street to Nana's apartment.

A Warm Day In March

Sean Lapointe had become a Boston Celtics fan, like his dad and great-grandmother, and the Celts were on TV on Sunday afternoon, March 8, 1987. The family gathered in Mrs. Martin's living room to watch the game and chat. They had coffee and a little something to eat. The Celtics lost a tough one to the Detroit Pistons, 122-119, in overtime. The outcome aside, it was a pleasant visit.

The Lapointes left about 4 P.M., and headed home. It was about a 10-minute walk to their house at 75 Union St., a large two-family that had been turned into a four-unit condominium — Karen's family helped with the purchase — in the comfortable, working-class neighborhood. It was a warm afternoon for early March.

At about 5:45 P.M., Natalie Howard, Mrs. Martin's daughter and Karen's aunt, and her husband, Earle, drove by Mayfair Gardens and saw Mrs. Martin putting the garbage out. "Should we stop?" the husband asked. "No, I'll call her when we get home," Natalie Howard said. Howard later called her mother twice, but got no answer. So she called the Lapointes at about 8 P.M. They were watching TV. Would Richard go over and check on Mother? Sure, Richard said. He walked over and knocked on Mrs. Martin's door. It felt warm, but he didn't think anything of that. He got no answer, so he walked over to the home of a neighbor he knew, Jeannette King. She let him use her phone. He called Karen and Natalie Howard, and said the lights were out and Mrs. Martin must have gone to bed.

She was a night owl. He was told to check again. He walked back to Mrs. Martin's apartment. This time the door was hot, and he could see smoke coming out from under the eaves. He went back to King's home, excited and out of breath, and dialed 911. Firefighters and police found the living room couch on fire, filling the apartment with smoke. Mrs. Martin was on the living room floor, unconscious. A volunteer firefighter dragged her out. She was pronounced dead shortly thereafter. The 88-year-old woman had been bound tightly around the neck and wrists, stabbed and sexually assaulted. The couch fire was one of three the assailant set in the apartment, apparently to destroy evidence.

Police interviewed dozens of people, including Richard and Karen Lapointe. They said they were at home from about 4:15 until Natalie

Howard called at 8 P.M. Although Richard Lapointe remained on the list of 26 suspects, investigators thought they knew who the killer was.

PEANUT BUTTER

Around the corner from Mayfair Gardens is a cozy neighborhood snug, Kelly's Pub and Restaurant. Shortly after Mrs. Martin's murder, police officers came into Kelly's with pictures. Had the owners seen any of these men?

Annette Kelehan, wife of Charles "Kelly" Kelehan, said yes. She pointed to a photo of a gaunt, dark-haired man and said he looked like a man who'd been in the bar the weekend Mrs. Martin was killed. The man was the notorious Frederick Rodney Merrill, known as "the peanut butter bandit" because he'd once broken out of jail with a gun slipped to him in a jar of peanut butter.

Merrill, now 46, is much less romantic a figure than his nickname might suggest. He is a career criminal with countless burglaries, robberies, and other crimes, as well as four prison escapes. He is also charged in at least two sexual assaults. His connection to the Martin case was tantalizing.

He was seen in the bar. He fit the general description of someone seen running across North Main Street away from Mayfair Gardens shortly after 8 P.M. the night of the killing. More significant, he was arrested three days later for sexually assaulting a 55-year-old woman in South Windsor, less than three miles away.

While Merrill was in jail for the South Windsor incident, Manchester police tried to connect him to the Martin killing. Before they could, Merrill bid adieu. In August, he escaped from the maximum security section of Somers prison. He was found in Canada, and jailed in Toronto for nine crimes, including sexual assault. He escaped again, was recaptured, and is now in a Canadian federal prison in Quebec province.

Manchester police eventually dropped Merrill as a suspect because of his blood type. There were two bits of forensic evidence found in Bernice Martin's apartment. One was a drop of blood on an envelope that may or may not have belonged to the assailant; the other was a semen stain on the bedspread that probably belonged to the assailant. Tests showed both were left by someone with type A blood. Merrill is type AB negative.

That left the cupboard bare. Murders are relatively rare in Manchester, especially rape-murders of kindly old ladies. The Martin family, which included a state police trooper and other solid citizens, wanted it solved.

About a year after the crime, local officers worked with the FBI's Behavioral Sciences Unit in Quantico, Virginia, to create an "offender's profile." The unit, noted in Thomas Harris's novel *The Silence of the Lambs,* analyzes a crime scene for characteristics of the criminal. It can, for example, sometimes be determined how experienced the criminal was from how he committed the crime.

Although Manchester police wouldn't open their files or comment for this story because the conviction is being appealed, persons close to the case said the profile of Bernice Martin's killer was of a young man, a loner, possibly a member of her family who lived nearby, and knew Mrs. Martin and where she lived, a man who was socially inept and had a weak self-image, a man who had problems with overbearing women.

The group that assembled the profile was headed by a New York State Police lieutenant, John Edward Grant, who was spending the year with the FBI. Grant stayed with the case through Lapointe's arrest. The profile, however, didn't produce an instant suspect. After the case had gone unsolved for two years, it was assigned to a new man.

Paul Lombardo, a 12-year veteran of the force, had been a detective for a little more than two years, and was on his second homicide investigation. He is a tough, dark-haired, no-nonsense, hard-driving cop in the Joe Friday mold.

After reviewing the offender profile and the case file, Lombardo started interviewing the people involved. He interviewed Natalie Howard, and then, on June 8, he interviewed Richard Lapointe.

After that, he stopped interviewing suspects. He believed Lapointe was the killer. He now turned his efforts to proving it.

If he is right, Lombardo should be credited with a brilliant, 221B Baker St. piece of intuitive police work. Because despite all the stuff on the police station walls, Lombardo had nothing to prove Lapointe killed Mrs. Martin. He did learn that Lapointe had type A blood, like that found in the victim's apartment. But so does about 41 percent of the population.

Lombardo declined to comment for this story, but testified that he settled on Lapointe because the little man acted strange and did a number of suspicious things. Lombardo said when he called Lapointe in June to speak to him about the murder, Lapointe answered, "Why, am I a suspect?" Lombardo found this response unusual. When asked if he'd committed the murder, Lapointe's denial was "passive," not the "very strong affirmative objection you would expect." He said Lapointe assumed a "runner's position" while being questioned — that is, he had his feet pointed toward the door.

Lombardo took this as an indication of guilt. Lombardo knew he needed more for a conviction. He called Grant, who by now was back in New York. Opinions vary on how useful offender profiles are, but Lombardo was a believer. He asked Grant if Lapointe could have been the killer.

Didn't Lapointe have an alibi? Grant asked. Lombardo said he could defeat the alibi with a witness. Even though some of the profile doesn't fit Lapointe — he was neither young nor a loner — Grant said Lapointe would be a "very interesting" possibility.

Working with Grant and the Hartford County State's Attorney office, Lombardo set up the sting on the Fourth of July, when he knew Lapointe would have a day off. They'd display the phony evidence props. Lombardo would interrogate Lapointe. Another detective, Michael Morrissey, would go to the Lapointe home and interview Karen Lapointe.

CAN I GO TO THE BATHROOM?

The interrogation of Richard Lapointe began about 4 P.M. In a second-floor office, Lombardo began by telling Lapointe that the cops had plenty of proof that he did it, knew that he did it, had his fingerprints on a knife found at the scene, and now wanted to know why. It's not illegal, nor is it unheard of, for police to lie to a suspect or even display phony evidence.

Lapointe denied committing the murder, but eventually asked Lombardo if it were possible for a person to do such a crime and then black out and not remember it.

Lombardo said it was possible.

After an hour or two — neither man could remember exactly — Lapointe gave Lombardo a two-sentence statement: "On March 8 I was responsible for Bernice Martin's death and it was an accident. My mind went blank."

Lapointe then went to the bathroom. Afterward, he recanted the confession, saying he gave it so he would be allowed to go to the bathroom.

Lapointe asked about using the phone to call his wife or a lawyer. Lombardo said he pushed the phone in front of Lapointe, but didn't leave the room or offer any other assistance. He said Lapointe never picked up the phone. Lapointe said when he asked about calling a lawyer, Lombardo told him: "Later." It's unclear if Lapointe understood why he needed a lawyer. He said he asked because he'd seen it done on a TV show.

Lapointe said Lombardo "played games" to get him to confess. "I'd say, 'You just want me to say I did it,' and he'd say, 'See, you just said you did it.'" Lombardo kept talking. As the evening wore on, Lapointe dictated another confession:

> "On March 8, 1987, I went to visit Bernice Martin with my wife and son. We left the apartment in the late afternoon and went home. I left my house some time after that to take the dog for a walk. I was at Bernice Martin's apartment with the dog. We were both there together and the time was right. I probably made a pass at her and she said no. So I hit her and I strangled her. If the evidence shows I was there and that I killed her, then I killed her, but I don't remember being there.
>
> "I made a pass at Bernice because she was a nice person and I thought that I could get somewhere with her. She was like a grandmother to me, that I never had."

LIAR ON THE WIRE

As Lombardo interviewed Richard, Michael Morrissey, a veteran detective, arrived at the Lapointe home and began questioning Karen. Morrissey wore a "wire," or hidden microphone, and secretly tape-recorded this conversation with the help of his brother, officer Joseph Morrissey, who was outside in a patrol car.

The transcript makes it obvious that Michael Morrissey lied to

Karen numerous times: He said DNA testing had proved Richard was the killer, that he cut his hand and left a drop of blood in the apartment, that neighbors had heard screaming and seen Richard carrying something into the apartment.

Morrissey tried to coax Karen into turning on her husband, and threatened her with the loss of her son.

"Richard is going to get arrested, OK? I don't want that to happen to you, because you're going to have to deal with somebody else taking care of your son. Do you know that?" Morrissey said.

Despite this, the fragile woman stuck to her story. "That's not Richard," she said, twice, as Morrissey described how Richard might have done the crime. Did Richard ever hit their son? "Never." How did he treat you? "Fine."

Karen added one element she'd forgotten the first time. She said on the night of the killing, Richard went out to walk the dog at about 5 P.M., before dinner, but was back "within 20 minutes." She was emphatic about it, saying they had dinner at 5:30 and Richard was there.

Since Bernice Martin was seen alive at 5:45 P.M., this should have been an alibi. But Morrissey didn't see it that way. He returned to headquarters and took over the interrogation of Richard Lapointe. The pitch was that Morrissey had broken the news to the wife, and she was supporting him and wanted him to talk, so now he could tell the whole story.

Curiously, even though Morrissey wore the wire when talking to Karen Lapointe, and he and his brother went directly to the station afterwards, there is no tape or transcript of Morrissey's interrogation of Lapointe. Taping is not required by law, but is standard practice in some jurisdictions. One officer, Wayne Rautenberg, testified he thought there was such a tape of the Lapointe interview, but none ever surfaced. What did surface, after another four hours of questioning, was a third confession.

It starts with the family's visit to Mrs. Martin's apartment, and their walk home at 4 P.M.

> "After being home awhile I left to walk the dog. I then walked back up to Bernice's apartment and she invited me in. We each had a cup of coffee (I think Bernice had tea) and I sat

on the couch. I remember having my matches and my smoking pipe in my jacket pocket.

"After my coffee I went into the bathroom (which is located off the bedroom). When I came out Bernice was in the bedroom combing her hair. She was wearing a pink house coat type of outer wear with no bra (I could see her breasts when she bent over). I grabbed her with my hand around her waist area. When I did that she pushed me. I threw her on the bed and took off her underwear because I wanted to have intercourse with her. I got my penis inside her for a few strokes and then pulled out and masturbated. I did cum on the bed spread when I was finished. I had already thrown her underwear on the right side of the bed. After the sex she said she was going to tell my wife Karen. I then went to the kitchen and got a steak knife with a hard plastic brown handle and stabbed Bernice in the stomach while she was laying on the couch. The rest of the incident I do not recall although I admit to having strangled her."

(When he later testified about the confession, Morrissey said Lapointe demonstrated how he strangled Mrs. Martin with both hands.)

Finally, after midnight, Lapointe was presented with a third interrogator, Capt. Joseph Brooks, head of the detective division. Brooks knew Lapointe because both frequented My Brother's Place.

Brooks said he was brought in because Lapointe "continued to vacillate." That is, he'd give a statement, then recant and say he was just parroting what they told him, saying what they wanted to hear so he could go to the bathroom or go home. Police insisted that Lapointe was always free to get up and walk out of the station. But even Brooks testified that Lapointe told him he didn't know he wasn't under arrest and could leave.

After Morrissey left her home, Karen Lapointe called her mother, Margaret Dana of Farmington. Dana called Karen's brother, Kenneth Martin of Wallingford. They met at Karen's house. At 10 P.M., Dana and Kenneth Martin went to the police station. They wanted to find out what was happening with Richard, to see if he needed a lawyer and take him home if possible. Dana testified a police lieutenant told her that he couldn't interrupt the questioning. He also said that Richard had been told about getting a lawyer, but had said he didn't want one.

No one told Lapointe his family members were there. After a half hour, an officer suggested they go home, and told them he would call when Richard could be picked up. Kenneth Martin called again at midnight. The police put him off, again. Asked why she didn't push for a lawyer for Richard, Dana said, "We thought he was just being interviewed. We had no idea what transpired that night."

Lapointe told Brooks he was cold, hungry and tired. Finally, well after 1 A.M., they let Lapointe go home. It's unclear if Brooks had complete command and control on the Lapointe case. He testified he didn't know Morrissey secretly taped the interview with Karen Lapointe.

Regardless of who called the shots, it seems unusual that they'd let a confessed, sadistic sex killer go home to a wife with cerebral palsy and a small child. Would they have let a Fred Merrill go home?

Lapointe got up and went to work the next morning. He was arrested that evening, after Lombardo had finished the application for an arrest warrant. Although Lombardo claimed to have other evidence linking Lapointe to the crime, what he really had were the three confessions he and Morrissey sweated out of Lapointe over nine hours the night before.

The elemental question here is whether Lapointe would confess to a heinous crime he didn't commit, just because it would get him a trip to the bathroom or because he couldn't stand up to authority, or because he thought he had to do it to be allowed to go home.

Do mentally handicapped persons sometimes confess to crimes they haven't committed? Unfortunately, *yes*. Robert Perske of Darien — an author who is a former pastor, a former mental retardation caseworker and administrator and a past president of the Connecticut Association for Retarded Citizens — has written a book about it, titled *Unequal Justice?*

He writes that many people with mental disabilities become hugely reliant on authority figures and try inordinately to please them, even if it means giving wrong answers and incriminating themselves. He said such people look for clues from interrogators on what to say, and often don't understand abstract concepts such as waiving rights.

"They often think it is waving to the right, or something like that," Perske writes. He took a close interest in the Lapointe trial.

Unfortunately for Lapointe, he wasn't on the jury.

CHANGE FOR A FIVE

As his trial approached in Superior Court in Hartford, Lapointe drew two very good public defenders, Patrick J. Culligan and Christopher M. Cosgrove, and a well-respected judge in David M. Barry. He also drew one of the toughest, most intimidating prosecutors in the system, Rosita M. Creamer.

Culligan and Cosgrove first filed a motion to throw out Lapointe's confessions. In a seven-week hearing before the judge that began in December of 1991, the public defenders tried to show the confessions were coerced and not voluntary, as required by law, and that Lapointe was really in custody and deserving of more legal safeguards than he received.

After several widely known cases in the 1960s, most notably *Miranda vs. Arizona* in 1966, a series of rules have been created to protect a suspect's right against self-incrimination, or, conversely, to prevent police officers from forcing confessions from suspects.

These rules give suspects a right to remain silent or stop talking at any time, and a right to a lawyer. But these rights only fully apply to a person in custody, and custody is sometimes an elusive concept.

Police are supposed to have probable cause to take someone into custody. But they can ask someone to come in voluntarily, as they did with Lapointe, and ask about a crime.

Culligan and Cosgrove argued that police went too far and held Lapointe in custody and coerced him to confess. They said letting him go home after he confessed was a ploy to make it look as if he hadn't been in custody.

A reasonable person is in custody, the State Supreme Court has held, "if in view of all surrounding circumstances" he believed "he was not free to leave."

Lapointe's lawyers said a person with Lapointe's limitations would have been too intimidated to leave or to resist police pressure to confess. Their argument turned on the depth of Lapointe's limitations.

His lawyers called a psychologist, Anne Phillips, and a psychiatrist, Dr. Kenneth Selig, who supported their contention and testified Lapointe was a mentally damaged man, vulnerable and gullible.

Phillips said Lapointe had "no ability to challenge figures of authority," and said if he were told something was true he'd think it was true. She said passive responses were to be expected from him, and shouldn't be seen as signs of guilt. Lapointe had intelligence, she said, but, because of his brain damage, couldn't use it to make sense of the world.

Along with the experts, Lapointe's lawyers paraded in a host of Manchester people who knew Lapointe. They described him as a jolly, meek "Mr. Peepers" man who was "slow," "not all there," "very simple," "mildly retarded" and — most commonly — "childlike" or "a child in a man's body." Many witnesses used similar words for Karen Lapointe as well.

Tom Moriarty, a manager at Andy's Foodtown market when Lapointe worked there as a bundleboy, said Lapointe believed everything he was told. One day when the store was out of bananas, Lapointe kept demanding to know why. To kid around, Moriarty said he'd forgotten to water the banana tree in the back room, and there were no bananas on it. Lapointe believed him.

Witnesses said numbers were very difficult for Lapointe. James Higgins said he once bought a beer from Lapointe when he was tending bar at the Knights of Columbus. He said he gave Lapointe a $5 bill and got more than $15 in change.

Creamer didn't let this stand. She methodically attacked the expert witnesses, as she would later do in front of the jury. She emphasized that Lapointe, whatever his shortcomings, was heading a family and holding a job.

Worse, for Lapointe, he scored 92 on an IQ test, putting him only in the 30th percentile, but still in the lower part of the average range. That he did so well was a surprise to all who knew him, but it helped Barry decide the confession was voluntary, and that Lapointe knew what he was doing. He denied the motion.

Perhaps that was inevitable. "If the cops don't screw up the Miranda warnings, and today they are trained not to, then it's very tough to suppress a confession. There's a lot of pressure on a judge to get it to a jury," said Hartford lawyer Hubert Santos, one of the region's most widely known criminal defense lawyers. Gerace concurred: "Getting a confession suppressed is next to impossible."

Lapointe not only lost his motion, he lost his family and his in-laws.

When he was first arrested, the Martin family supported Richard. It hadn't occurred to them that he might be the killer. "I was very shocked; it had never entered my mind," Natalie Howard told me. But by the time the case came to court, the family appeared to have been won over by the police and prosecution.

Elizabeth Martin, Karen's stepmother and one of the few family members who stood by Richard, said she would have come to the hearing from upstate New York to testify as a character witness, except other family members gave her the impression that "the evidence against him was overwhelming."

Karen filed for divorce, and reclaimed her maiden name. She was one of the last witnesses at the hearing to suppress the confession, and she weakened her previous statements.

She'd said several times earlier that Richard stayed home after he came back from walking the dog, before 5:30 P.M., on the night of the killing. This time she said that from 6:15 or 6:30 P.M. to about 7 P.M., she was upstairs getting her son ready for bed, so she wasn't sure whether Richard was home then.

When she and Sean came downstairs, she said, Richard was there, watching TV, not sweating or bleeding, looking and acting as he had before.

While she testified, Karen appeared to look away when Richard looked at her. At one point, when the subject of Richard's disabilities came up, Karen blurted, "There's nothing wrong with Richard."

Lapointe's lawyers now felt Karen had turned on her husband, become a potential liability, a loose cannon. They didn't call her to testify again.

GUILTY

With the confession in evidence, Lapointe's lawyers were forced to attack it again. At his trial last spring, they brought in Phillips again and another psychiatrist, Dr. Donald Grayson. Grayson said he found Lapointe's story that he signed the confession to go to the bathroom and get himself out of a stressful situation "quite believable."

He also noted that Lapointe had a certain body of knowledge — he does children's crossword puzzles and has memorized the state capitals. This may be why he scored as well as he did on IQ tests. Grayson called this "ice cream knowledge," nice to have but not useful in solving the problems of day-to-day living.

But Creamer, who Hartford County State's Attorney John Bailey calls the best cross-examiner of psychiatric experts in the state, lived up to her reputation. She blasted an apparently minor calculation error by Phillips, and shook Grayson's testimony with a series of hypothetical questions: Would he change his mind if he knew Lapointe had signed a detailed confession? Would he reconsider his opinion if he knew Lapointe provided police with details only the killer could have known? Grayson conceded that he might.

One juror, Carol Millet, later told me that Creamer "clouded" the expert testimony and "put doubt in our minds" about it.

Lapointe took the stand and said several times he didn't kill Bernice Martin. He signed the three confessions, he said, so the officers would let him go home. Creamer shook him with a fierce cross-examination. He seemed uncertain and confused about some events on the evening of Mrs. Martin's death, such as who he called after his first attempt to check on Mrs. Martin. Then she bore in on the confession. "If your desire was to be thought not guilty, how did you think you would advance that by providing ... confessions to the murder?" Creamer asked.

"I have no idea," Lapointe replied.

Those who support Lapointe saw the cross-examination as another example of his inability to stand up to authority figures and his inclination to tell such people what they want to hear. The jury viewed his testimony differently — as the squirming of a guilty man. Deliberations lasted only one hour.

"The confession was at least 75 percent of it," jury foreman Michael Palin said of the guilty verdict. He and others didn't believe Lapointe would confess so he could go to the bathroom or go home. They also believed the police, as most jurors do. Juror Eleanor Stinson said she found officers Lombardo and Morrissey "businesslike and professional" on the stand.

The jurors heard 11 weeks of exhaustive testimony. They appeared to pay close attention, and examined dozens of exhibits. The several jurors I interviewed seemed mindful of their responsibility to be fair. Margaret Dana, Karen's mother, told me her family was "comfortable" with the verdict.

Why are so many others uncomfortable with it?

A criminal defendant is presumed innocent. Accordingly, the U.S. Supreme Court in *In re Winship* has held he cannot be convicted "except upon proof beyond a reasonable doubt of every fact necessary to constitute the crime." Other cases have held reasonable doubt is a "square and honest doubt," a doubt growing out of the "evidence or lack of evidence," a doubt for which "you can state a reason."

Because of trial tactics and the rules of evidence, the jury did not hear everything. Combining at least three important pieces of information the jurors did not hear with much that they did, and talking with some people who didn't testify, I believe there are several square and honest reasons to doubt Lapointe's guilt.

THE CASE FOR LAPOINTE

Whoever raped and murdered Bernice Martin was a raging, violent maniac. Richard Lapointe is a meek and timid man who'd never struck his wife or child.

"There was no violence in him," said Joe Siracuse, who knew Lapointe and runs a shoe repair business in Burr Corner.

"If he was walking his dog and the dog stopped, he wouldn't even jerk the chain to get it moving again," said Charles Kelehan, the pub owner.

"He'd get agitated once in a while, but the extent of what he'd do if he was really mad was bang a few dishes," said Jack McTighe, his boss at Friendly's. "He was a strange guy, but not a violent one."

Did Lapointe change his personality for an hour, and then change back?

Unlikely people do commit crimes from time to time. Priests molest boys, or judges steal money. But people who know Lapointe don't think he had the mental or physical ability to commit this crime and then not tell anyone about it.

Jo-Ann McTighe, wife of Jack, often gave Lapointe rides to and from work. "I had him in the car so many times — it's just not possible he did this. He didn't have the mentality. He isn't smart enough. He never covered up anything he did; he couldn't."

Whoever committed the crime set fires to cover it up. "I can't see Richard being able to think of that," said Peter Engelbrecht, who worked with Lapointe at Friendly's, and now works for the Manchester Association for Retarded Citizens.

Lapointe was terribly clumsy. He frequently cut himself. He had trouble with simple tasks such as stocking supermarket shelves or making a sandwich. Jack McTighe once tried to teach him to make sandwiches. Lapointe had a bandage over a cut on his hand. It fell into a seafood sandwich and he left it there. So much for that.

In a sense, officer Lombardo was right. Lapointe's behavior was strange. But it was consistent with the way he always behaved. Lombardo found it odd that Lapointe asked, "Am I a suspect?" In the two years and four months between the crime and his arrest, Lapointe had asked other officers how the case was going, and if he was a suspect.

That's what he did. If he perceived someone as an authority figure — such as Jack McTighe or other bosses he'd had, or Karen's father, Bill Martin — he peppered them with questions. The case was important to the family, so Lapointe always asked about it. His wife sometimes scolded him about pestering police officers.

According to testimony in the trial, a neighbor had complained that Lapointe looked in her window, like a Peeping Tom. Lapointe said he was out walking his dog when he saw the woman in the window, and that he moved on. Several people said he stared at people in restaurants or other places. It was something else he did.

If his looking in windows means there's some voyeurism in him, and this isn't certain, it's still very different from being a rapist. "A voyeur traditionally is someone who doesn't want to make contact," said John Nolte, a Hartford psychologist who followed the Lapointe trial and believes Lapointe innocent.

A juror found it suspicious that Lapointe didn't call 911 right away, when he sensed that Mrs. Martin's door was warm. But according to McTighe and others, Lapointe does what his wife or his boss tells him. He was told to call his wife and her aunt, and he did.

While the jurors found Lapointe had some limitations, they still believed him capable of the crime. But could he have done it in the time allotted?

THE TIME FRAME

The jury never got to hear Karen Lapointe. Even though she seemed to Richard's lawyers to have turned on their client, it's possible, in retrospect, that she could still have helped his cause. Because even after she divorced Richard and weakened his alibi, she still provided a time frame in which it is almost impossible for Richard to have committed the crime.

She said he was back from walking the dog by 5:30 on the night of the killing, when Mrs. Martin was still alive. She doesn't say Richard left the house again, only that he was alone downstairs for 30 to 45 minutes, from 6:15 or 6:30 P.M. to about 7 P.M., when she and Sean came downstairs to watch a TV show.

That means that in 30 to 45 minutes, Richard Lapointe, a man who is slow and slow-witted, weak and a legendary klutz, had to take a 10-minute walk to Bernice Martin's apartment, have coffee with her, rape her, bind her, stab her, set the apartment on fire, take a 10-minute walk home, and sit down to watch TV, in the same clothes, not sweating or bleeding, looking as if he never left.

If Karen told the truth about her family's activities that evening, it's very hard to believe Richard guilty. Was she lying? She told basically the same story on four occasions. She didn't change it despite tremendous pressure from Detective Morrissey the night Richard was taken to police headquarters, nor did she change it in the suppression hearing, after she seemed to have turned against him. They went home. Richard walked the dog but was back at 5:30. The family had a meatloaf dinner, ending at 6:15 or 6:30 P.M. Sean and Karen went upstairs. Richard was there at 7 P.M. when they came downstairs. He was there at 8 P.M. when Karen's aunt, Natalie Howard, called.

Lapointe's lawyers mentioned the time frame problem several times, but didn't make it the centerpiece of the defense. Cosgrove used it in his summation to the jury as one element in a broad argument that there was no evidence to prove Lapointe committed the murder.

THE WARRANT

Much was made, on the arrest warrant and at the trial, of specific facts that Lapointe provided to police that only the killer would have known. These facts were supposed to be additional proof, beyond the confession, of Lapointe's guilt. They prove nothing. Analyzing them one by one, they are all either false or were known to more people than the killer.

Lombardo's big, alibi-busting witness putting Richard Lapointe

at the scene was Jeannette King, the 80-year-old neighbor. He says in
the warrant that King saw Richard walking his dog at about 7 P.M.
near Mrs. Martin's apartment on the night of the killing.

That is not how she testified in court. King said she never saw
Richard walking his dog. She only saw him come to her door twice,
one visit a few minutes from the other, asking to use the phone.
Unfortunately for Lapointe, she seemed confused about the time he
came to her door.

She told officer Kendall Keyes the night of the murder that
Lapointe came around 8 P.M. In court, she said it was a little after 7
P.M., noting that she could pinpoint the time because the sun was still
up. But sunset that day was at 5:49 P.M., and it was completely dark by
6:20 P.M. Nevertheless, she was emphatic that he came to her door
only two times — just as Lapointe said he did. Since the 911 call was
logged at 8:27 P.M., the 8 P.M. estimate is more likely. In any event, she
didn't see him walking the dog. Curiously, neither did anyone else at
the complex, even though lots of people saw him leave at about 4 P.M.
with his family, and nearly everyone in the busy complex knew Richard Lapointe.

The jury never heard Keyes testify about King's first statement
about the time of Lapointe's visit. He made the statement at the suppression hearing, and prosecutors, claiming hearsay, were able to keep
it out of the trial.

In the warrant, Lombardo says a friend of Karen's called the next
day to offer condolences, and got Richard on the phone. She said
Richard told her that Mrs. Martin had been raped. Lombardo says
this fact wasn't known until the autopsy was completed that afternoon, and that the information was not released to the family for a
year. Thus, Lombardo concludes, Lapointe appeared to have direct
knowledge of the sexual assault even before the police department
did.

The rape may not have been officially confirmed, but when a
half-naked bound woman is dragged from a crime scene, the specula-
tion of sexual assault is almost inevitable.

Jack McTighe went over to see Richard that day, to console him.
He said Richard told him a firefighter or ambulance attendant told
him Mrs. Martin had been raped.

Elizabeth Martin, Karen's stepmother, called the Manchester police that day and got Captain Brooks on the phone. She said Brooks told her that Mrs. Martin had been raped.

Finally, Manchester deputy fire marshal Christopher Marvin said one of his fire inspectors went to the hospital that night and was told Mrs. Martin was raped. "In addition, it was determined that Martin had also been sexually assaulted," Marvin wrote in his report. Lapointe doesn't seem to be the only one who heard about the rape.

The warrant says Karen Lapointe told Morrissey that when Richard left to walk the dog, he took an unusual route, toward Mrs. Martin's apartment. The transcript of her taped interview says the opposite: that it was not an unusual route to walk the dog, and it wasn't the way they usually went to Mrs. Martin's apartment. When presented with the transcript on the witness stand during the trial, Morrissey admitted he was wrong, but insisted the rest of his report was accurate.

This negates another specific point in the warrant that Karen Lapointe and Jeannette King confirmed that Richard walked his dog to Mrs. Martin's apartment. Neither did.

Lombardo says Lapointe admitted stabbing Mrs. Martin in the abdomen. He said this information was never released to the public, so it was another fact only the killer would know. But Lapointe and others were there when Mrs. Martin's body was brought out of her apartment. She was lying on her back and there was a big red stain on the cloth covering her, in the middle of her body. Lapointe made this observation to the police officer who interviewed him on the night if the killing. Everyone who was there knew Mrs. Martin was stabbed in the stomach area. Lapointe couldn't see the 10 stab wounds in her back. But he didn't admit to causing those.

Lombardo says Lapointe confessed to setting fire to the couch while Mrs. Martin was on it, and says evidence showed Mrs. Martin was on the couch when the fire started. But Dr. Arkady Katsnelson, the assistant state medical examiner who performed the autopsy, testified Mrs. Martin's body was not in direct contact with flame, so it was not on the burning couch.

The detective mentions Lapointe's statements about having coffee and about Mrs. Martin brushing her hair, and says photos showed coffee cups and a hair brush. The coffee cups may have been from the early afternoon; a hairbrush on a woman's dresser is not uncommon.

Lapointe is said to have admitted using a steak knife with a brown handle to stab Mrs. Martin, and Lombardo says such a knife was found in the apartment. That's not entirely accurate. A steak knife blade was found in the apartment, and a bag of burned crumbs was identified as a knife handle. But it's not on the list of evidence that was analyzed by the state forensic lab. If the handle was brown, it isn't an uncommon color for steak knife handles, and Lapointe would have been familiar with Mrs. Martin's cutlery.

Finally, the warrant says no sperm were found in the semen sample, and that this is consistent with the fact that Lapointe had had a vasectomy. It really proves nothing. Some semen samples don't have sperm in them, because sperm isn't evenly distributed in semen, and heat over 120 degrees destroys sperm, several experts said. Fire officials testified the heat in the apartment fire was between 500 and 600 degrees.

What Lombardo really had was the confession. The confession has so many inconsistencies that it is almost as if Lapointe confessed to the wrong crime.

Wrong Theory?

Let's dismiss the first two confessions as ludicrous and oxymoronic. A rational person cannot admit to having done something he can't remember doing. Let's go to the third confession that Lapointe gave to Detective Morrissey.

In this one, Lapointe leaves to walk the dog, goes over to Mrs. Martin's apartment, has coffee, then goes to the bathroom. When he comes out, Mrs. Martin is sitting in a housecoat with no bra, brushing her hair. Lapointe can see her breasts when she bends over.

He assaults her on the bed. He gets his penis in for a few strokes, then withdraws it and masturbates on the bedspread. She tells him she's going to tell his wife. So he goes and gets a knife and stabs her on the couch, strangles her with his hands, and then doesn't remember anything else.

Family members say Mrs. Martin was a proper woman who wouldn't have appeared as Lapointe said.

Lapointe is supposed to have said, "I had already thrown her underwear on the right side of the bed." Would Richard Lapointe, a man with a weak memory, remember a detail such as that almost two and a half years later? Or is it something police fed him, because it happened to correspond to a photo of the scene?

More importantly, the autopsy showed so many cuts and bruises in and around the vagina and urethra that Katsnelson says the rape was most likely done with a blunt instrument.

Then there is the location of the body. Police believed Mrs. Martin was raped and stabbed, then placed on the living room couch, which was then set on fire. So says the warrant. This somewhat corresponds to Lapointe's confession — he says he stabbed Martin on the couch — but not to what experts believe actually happened.

Subsequent testimony by Katsnelson and others showed Mrs. Martin wasn't on the couch. She was found across the room, six or eight feet from the couch. That led to a new theory: that Mrs. Martin was raped and stabbed in the bedroom, and then somehow crawled outside the bedroom door, where she lost consciousness.

Finally, Morrissey was clear that Lapointe admitted strangling Mrs. Martin with both hands. Katsnelson says Mrs. Martin was not strangled with two hands. "This is not a manual strangulation," he said. He said because of the kinds of bruises present, it was strangulation by compression, most likely by a blunt object being pushed against the right side of her neck.

Thus, the salient elements of the crime didn't happen the way Lapointe confessed to them. Curiously, his confession did correspond to the police theory of the crime. Is it possible, as Lapointe claims, that police officers put words in his mouth? Or that he confessed to what he read in the paper? Or some combination of the two? The facts known only to the killer were also known to the police.

IF NOT LAPOINTE, WHO?

Fred Merrill would seem to be eliminated by his blood type. I reached him by phone in a Canadian federal prison, and asked him if he committed this crime. He said no, and that he escaped from Somers and fled to Canada because he feared police would blame him for the Martin murder as well as the South Windsor assault.

I said people in the area identified his picture. He said he had been indulging in intoxicants, and couldn't be completely sure about his actions. "When you do a lot of drugs and alcohol you're capable of anything," he observed. But he said he was pretty sure he didn't do the Martin murder.

If Merrill is out because of his blood type, another suspect should have stayed in because of his blood type. A young man named Brad Thomas, arrested and charged in another rape and burglary in the area in 1988, was at first a strong suspect in the case. Thomas, like Lapointe, had type A blood.

Thomas was eliminated because there was evidence of sperm in the 1988 rape he was arrested for, and none in the Martin case. But as testimony showed, the fire most likely would have destroyed any sperm that may have been present, or there may not have ever been any sperm in the sample that was tested.

So Thomas should have remained a suspect. He hanged himself in his jail cell after his arrest. Lapointe's lawyers were prevented by rules of evidence from presenting the Thomas situation to the jury.

There may be another strong possibility. One reason the FBI profile liked Lapointe was that he knew where Mrs. Martin's apartment was, and why would a stranger pick this particular place?

But the Martin home had been burglarized a year earlier. Someone knew it. When fire fighters entered the apartment on the day of her death, they found the back door open.

Finally, in the year before the Martin killing, a 76-year-old woman was sexually assaulted in the Rockville section of Vernon. She described her assailant as a young man in his teens or early 20s. The case was never solved. Police say there were "some similarities" between the Rockville and South Windsor cases and the killing of Bernice Martin.

EPILOGUE

A jury doesn't have to tie up every loose end in a case, yet the seemingly substantial inconsistencies in the Lapointe case made no impact. One juror seemed to blame them on Lapointe. "He's like a child, he can convince himself he didn't do it," she said, "but anyone can commit a murder. He has a mental problem, but he did function in society."

Margaret Dignoti, executive director of the Connecticut Association for Retarded Citizens, attended much of the trial. She's convinced Lapointe was found guilty because many people think persons with mental problems are capable of sudden, violent acts.

"But that's mythology," she said. "There's absolutely no data to back that up." Culligan said the hardest part of defending Lapointe was getting the jury to see the real Richard. "He's not a child, he's an adult with some childish tendencies. His brain developed abnormally so he is totally idiosyncratic. But it's hard to get people to see this."

For example, the jury didn't believe Lapointe would confess just to go to the bathroom. But, said Culligan, at several key points in the trial, when he was literally fighting for Lapointe's life, Lapointe would lean over and ask when he could go to the bathroom.

It is possible what the jury didn't hear could have affected the outcome. They didn't hear time-frame testimony from Karen Lapointe, testimony from officer Kendall Keyes that Jeannette King never saw Richard Lapointe until about 8 P.M. on the night of the murder, nor did they hear about the other suspects. They also never heard most of the people quoted in this story, such as Siracuse, Engelbrecht, the McTighes, Dignoti, Perske and Nolte.

Apart from the verdict remains the question of due process. Since confessions rarely get thrown out, and police testimony is almost always believed, Lapointe was all but cooked when he voluntarily walked into the police station.

"Of course he was in custody," said Gerace. "A guy like this isn't going to get up and walk out. Think how you feel when a police officer pulls you over."

That Gerace may be right is Lapointe's last hope. The public defender's office has appealed the case, specifically Judge Barry's decision not to throw out Lapointe's confession. Lapointe's supporters, who still meet and try to help him, aren't optimistic. They think the only real chance is finding another suspect.

Lapointe, who has been in custody since the day after he gave his confession in 1989, remains in Somers prison. He is much as he was in Manchester.

John Salo, educational psychologist at the prison, said Lapointe's reading level is mid-3rd grade to early 4th grade, making him functionally illiterate.

This means there's a serious question of whether he understood his Miranda rights in the two minutes Manchester police took to read them to him and have him sign a waiver.

Salo said Lapointe is taking the lowest level adult education class, but has trouble focusing on reading or listening for more than five or seven minutes at a time. He sometimes gets exhausted after one class. The other men in the class seem to like him. They kid and tease him about his absentmindedness and lack of energy, but seem to look out for him.

He jokes with them, sometimes about his own weak vision and poor hearing. Lapointe doesn't participate in the prison exercise activities, goes to church, reads the newspaper occasionally and watches a little TV. Salo, like the mental health experts who testified at the trial, described Lapointe as the kind of low-functioning person who is subservient to authority.

He wore brown khaki prison clothes the day I visited him in December. I looked into his big eyes, which don't seem to move together, and asked if he committed the murder.

"No, I did not," he said quietly, but not what I would call passively. "I got a bad deal." He was cheerful most of the time I was with him. He said the loss of his son was the worst part of it.

The props, the stuff the police hung on the walls, the "Mission Impossible" style sting the police prepared for Lapointe? It was probably more trouble than it was worth. Lapointe said he only remembered seeing the picture of Bernice Martin.

JUSTICE UNSERVED?

Connecticut is About to Witness the Appeal
of Another Murder Conviction
Based on a Questionable Confession

By **DONALD S. CONNERY**

Five years is a long time to spend behind bars for a crime you did not commit. Five years is longer than World War I, longer than America's march to victory in World War II, longer than most of our presidents have spent in the White House. And five years is all it takes for a boy to go from age 10 to age 15. Except that Richard Lapointe has not been allowed to see his only child growing up.

Not since July 4, 1989. That was the day Connecticut, "The Constitution State," once again succumbed to its peculiar addiction to inquisitions.

That was the day the Manchester police phoned to ask Lapointe if he would drop by for a talk. It wasn't a convenient time; he was preparing food for a family picnic. But they told him it wouldn't take long, and he was used to doing whatever people wanted him to do.

At the station, they read him his rights. Then they lied to him. They said that they had proof that he was a murderer.

Nine and a half hours later, police interrogators had his signature on three conflicting confessions. To their satisfaction, they had solved the mystery of the March 8, 1987, rape, stabbing, strangulation and attempted incineration of Bernice Martin of Manchester. She was a woman Richard adored, his wife's 88-year-old grandmother.

They had it in black and white: "If the evidence shows that I was there, and that I killed her, then I killed her, but I don't remember being there."

They even had a couple of pages of details, in their own typed words and handwriting, about how he had carried out the crime he could not remember.

Such as: "She was wearing a pink house coat type of outer wear with no bra." "I then went to the kitchen and got a steak knife with a hard plastic brown handle."

These were marvelously exact bits of information, more than two years after the event, supposedly uttered by a bewildered, exhausted, barely educated, brain-damaged, mentally disabled, hearing-impaired, sight-impaired, poorly coordinated, weak little man with a short attention span.

Their work done, the police then let the confessed rapist-murderer-arsonist go home to his family and his neighborhood.

Confused by this strange turn of events, Lapointe figured that the cops now realized that they had made a mistake. He had told them over and over again, until well past midnight, that he was innocent.

The police didn't seem to understand that he had simply been home with his family, watching television, at the time of the murder. It was a worried call from his wife's aunt that had sent him up to Martin's house to see if she was all right. When he found the place on fire, he called 911.

He had no idea of the peril facing him. He had not insisted on a lawyer earlier and he did not seek one now. If you're innocent, why do you need a lawyer?

He went to sleep. Then he put in a full day's work at his dishwashing job. They came for him that evening, July 5, 1989.

They put him in jail. He stayed there 2½ years. His wife divorced him. When he finally got his day in court, in proceedings that consumed another half-year of his life, two things happened:

A judge decided that the confessions had been made voluntarily under proper conditions by a man smart enough to understand his rights.

A jury, after an hour of discussion, found him guilty of all nine charges brought against him.

The jury was not overly troubled by discrepancies in the arrest warrant or the absence of motive, eyewitnesses, credible evidence or time enough for him to carry out a complicated crime and cover his tracks.

Both the hearing on the confessions and the subsequent trial were a triumph for the tough and intimidating lead prosecutor, Rosita Creamer.

Armed with a questionable test that put Lapointe's IQ at low-average 92, surprisingly high to all who know him, she made short work of the specialists who spoke of his childlike way of speaking or the consequences of hydrocephalus — fluid pressure on the brain — and the five operations that had been required to deal with it.

And so, on Sept. 8, 1992, Lapointe was sentenced to life in prison without parole plus 60 years. The prosecutors were disappointed. They had argued for the death penalty. He was 46 years old. His life, for all practical purposes, was over.

Now a nobody is about to become a somebody. The state's most prominent civil-rights attorney, John Williams, is taking over his appeal. Playwright Arthur Miller has chastised the Connecticut Bar Association for failing to protect the innocent. *60 Minutes* is investigating. Connecticut's justice system is going to be subjected to a blaze of media scrutiny and public attention not seen since the nationally publicized Peter Reilly nightmare of 1973-77.

I had never heard of Richard Lapointe until last August, when I received a letter from a group of citizens who had come together after his conviction to see what they could do to help him. They had been meeting every other Wednesday evening in the exotic setting of the community conference room of the Wethersfield Burger King.

They knew that I had written a book about the Reilly case and had played some role in exposing the elaborate State Police effort in 1977 to frame him a second time.

They knew that Reilly (now 39) owed his freedom to the Litchfield County people who had stood up for him from the start and had found professional help. Would I mind taking a look at the Hartford area's Lapointe case?

My first reaction to this horror story was astonishment that a case so similar to Reilly's should arise again in Connecticut. There were these important differences, however:

Reilly was a naive, compliant teenager. Lapointe was a simple, brain-damaged middle-aged man.

Reilly's was a "coerced-internalized" false confession. Lapointe's was "coerced-compliant." In other words, Reilly was led to doubt his own memory and believe himself guilty while Lapointe said he was guilty in order to end the ordeal. He wanted the badgering to stop. He wanted to go to the bathroom. He wanted to go home.

There is an audiotape of Reilly's eight-hour interrogation that reveals exactly how he was brainwashed. There is no audiotape or videotape record, as there should be, to help us understand how the Manchester police manipulated Lapointe.

My overall reaction to this case, however, has been along the lines of Yogi Berra's immortal phrase, "It's *déjà vu* all over again."

I have in mind all the instances that led California's *Sacramento Bee* in a 1990 nationwide survey of notorious false confession cases to focus more attention on Connecticut than any other state.

I have in mind all the times we either abused the guilty or prosecuted the innocent. From the 1950s to the late 1970s, during and after the reign of Sam Rome as Connecticut's most feared and famous detective, the State Police focused on confessions as the fastest way to solve crimes. Their more extreme tactics led to two U.S. Supreme Court rulings about violations of the constitutional protection against self-incrimination.

Suspects were held incommunicado and shuffled from one police barracks to another to keep them from their lawyers. They were tricked, bullied and browbeaten into making true or false admissions. One man confessed after Rome, known as a master at interrogation, led him to believe that the rubber cup of a scalp massager was a lie detector.

Municipal police departments — and the state's attorneys who ran the prosecutions — were often just as reckless in their treatment of suspects. In the 1973 case of Benjamin Miller, even Stalin's henchmen would have been impressed.

Miller was a schizophrenic postal clerk and street preacher who became the designated suspect in a series of black prostitute murders in the Stamford-Norwalk area. He was induced to confess. The authorities who pronounced the crimes solved at a huge press conference were then mortified when a state trooper came upon the actual killer strangling his latest victim.

Miller was quietly dispatched to an institution for the criminally insane while the murderer got a sweet deal: a few years in jail. John

Williams had to fight through four courts to finally free Miller after 15 years in captivity.

It is no wonder that William Styron, after personal experience with Reilly and two earlier cases of injustice, wrote that "the law's power is too often invested in the hands of mortal men who are corrupt, or, if not corrupt, stupid, or if not stupid then devious or lazy, and all of them capable of the most grievous mischief."

In the matter of Lapointe, there was no end to the mischief. It didn't help that the Manchester Police Department was in some state of discord at the time of his interrogation and arrest. There was no tight rein by the top officers on the less experienced investigators who were gung-ho to solve the Martin murder.

A low point was reached when a detective interviewed Karen Lapointe at home while Richard was being questioned at the station. When she gave no support to their theory that her husband had murdered her grandmother, the cop threatened her with the loss of her child if she did not cooperate.

But the overzealousness of investigators is an old story. What counts is the prosecutor's decision to accept or reject their work. Lapointe would be free today if Hartford County State's Attorney John M. Bailey, now chief state's attorney, and his prosecutors had applied anything like the skepticism about police work that Homer Cummings displayed in the celebrated case of *State vs. Israel* in 1924.

The Bridgeport police, investigating the slaying of a popular priest, gave prosecutor Cummings "iron-clad" evidence against a mentally retarded vagrant, Harold Israel. They not only had his full confession, they had a motive, excellent eyewitnesses and the gun in the suspect's pocket that had put the bullet in the priest's head.

When Cummings appeared in court to prosecute Israel, he amazed everyone by proclaiming the man's innocence. He had conducted his own investigation of the murder. Now he proceeded to demolish every single item of the false confession and fraudulent evidence.

Israel was set free. Cummings went on to become Franklin D. Roosevelt's attorney general.

It will be a long time, however, before Lapointe is set free. It has already taken two years since his trial just to get the transcripts typed. It may take another two years or more for the appeal process and a new trial.

In a more perfect world, of course, we would not have to depend, as Styron says, on "the will of ordinary people, in their ever astonishing energy and determination, to see true justice prevail over the law's dereliction." We would expect the state's highest authorities to find the quickest way possible to pluck an innocent man from prison.

But this won't happen. We will witness instead a massive effort in denial. Police and prosecutors do not admit mistakes. Nor do they apologize for mistakes. Nor do they suffer the consequences of their mistakes.

In this state, if you are a fatherless teenager who just lost his mother, or a mentally disturbed street preacher, or a mentally disabled dishwasher, watch out for the people who are supposed to protect you.

On the other hand, you may be surprised, as Richard Lapointe has been surprised, by the kindness of strangers. The new-found friends who visit him in prison these days have come upon something quite remarkable, like a story out of the Bible.

They say that Lapointe is doing all right. He cheerfully endures. They had feared that this 5-foot-4 "Mr. Magoo," as he has been taunted all his life, would be harassed by his jailers and victimized by the wolves who prey on the helpless.

Not so. He is being treated gently by his keepers. He is getting more consideration from lawbreakers than he ever got from our guardians of the law.

Connecticut's convicts are protecting him like a little brother. They are sheltering him like a lost lamb.

Because they know he doesn't belong there.

Journal Inquirer, Manchester, CT, January 13, 1995
Conclusion of a five-part series, "Tainted Justice"

LYING ACCEPTED INVESTIGATIVE TOOL

But Deception Throws Doubts on Confessions, Investigators' Credibility

By ALEX WOOD

If you lie to a police investigator, it can be a crime.

But if he lies to you, it's OK.

Letting the police lie to get the truth in criminal investigations is a concept that has gained wide acceptance in American law enforcement and in the nation's courts, including the Supreme Court.

Although courts have expressed some ambivalence on the subject, they have ruled that police interrogators may use outright lies as well as subtler forms of deception to extract confessions from criminal suspects. And such practices have been urged on police by writers of how-to-do-it manuals about interrogation.

In one of the best-known of these manuals, Fred E. Inbau and John E. Reid advise interrogators of suspects "whose guilt is definite or reasonably certain" to display an air of confidence in the suspect's guilt.

They go on to say that "the interrogator must give no indication that he is being influenced by what the subject may state in behalf of his innocence; this should be so even when the interrogator actually realizes the reasonable implication of possible innocence in some fact or evidence referred to by the subject."

Such advice makes clear that the police officer is expected to show more confidence in the suspect's guilt than he may actually have.

The Manchester police investigation of the murder of Bernice Martin — in particular the secretly made tape recording of Detective Michael Morrissey's July 4, 1989, interview with Karen Lapointe, wife of the suspect, Richard Lapointe — illustrates how such techniques are sometimes put into practice.

Morrissey later testified that he considered Karen Lapointe a "hostile" witness, and almost the first thing he told her was that police were sure her husband had murdered Martin, her grandmother.

That was a lie, and Morrissey proceeded to buttress it with other lies, claiming falsely that police had physical evidence and a confession proving her husband's guilt.

The 1969 U.S. Supreme Court decision that is considered the leading precedent on police deception devotes only two sentences to the issue. The decision deals with a confession obtained from an Oregon murder suspect after police told him falsely that his cousin had confessed to involvement in the crime.

The decision, written by Justice Thurgood Marshall, one of the court's leading liberals, says the police misrepresentation was relevant but "insufficient in our view to make this otherwise voluntary confession inadmissible."

The Richard Lapointe case and others like it raise many questions about that tolerant attitude toward lying by police. Among the most serious is whether lies told by the police may induce innocent people to confess falsely.

A Florida case from 1973 — in which the defendant was convicted — illustrates one obvious way that might happen.

The suspect, Jackson B. Burch, was interrogated for 5½ hours by five Palm Beach County sheriff's deputies about the death of 18-year-old Pamela Curry, whose body had been buried in a pump house by a sea wall.

Burch maintained his innocence in the face of repeated accusations and fabricated evidence. According to a Florida Supreme Court decision, he eventually agreed to take a lie-detector test but was given a fake one, then told it proved that he had lied in denying he had committed the murder.

Next a detective told Burch that he would decide whether to charge him with first-degree murder, which under Florida law carried the death penalty, or second-degree murder, which carried a seven- to 20-year prison sentence.

The detective advised Burch to consider those options when deciding whether he should confess and explain the circumstances of the crime, according to the court decision.

At that point, the court decision said, Burch did confess, though his admissions included a claim that he had been "mentally blanking out" during an assault on the girl with a pocket knife.

The Florida Supreme Court ruled that Burch's confession was admissible evidence at his trial because he had been given the standard "Miranda warnings" about his right to a lawyer and his right to remain silent. He also had been told he was free to leave the sheriff's office at any time.

Burch went to prison and remains there today. In the eyes of the law he is guilty.

But because of the official lies and manipulation, the case remains troubling. Burch was told in essence: "We've got you, and you could face the death penalty. But if you confess, you may be able to persuade us to send you to prison for as little as seven years."

Why should that kind of pressure work only on a guilty person?

MINDS TURNED INSIDE-OUT

Psychologists and other students of confessions say that even an innocent suspect sometimes may come to believe in his own guilt when an authority figure confronts him with assertions that the evidence is overwhelming. Expert call it a "coerced-internalized confession."

"The influence tactics routinely used in interrogations are sufficiently powerful to cause some innocent persons to at least temporarily come to believe that they have committed a serious crime," Richard Ofshe, a sociology professor at the University of California at Berkeley, wrote in a 1989 paper.

Ofshe is one of the country's best-known students of false confessions, brainwashing, and "recovered" memories, which often involve claims that a person was abused as a child.

Claims that the suspect blacked out recollections of the crime often figure prominently in accounts of seriously disputed confessions.

Police generally view suspects' blackout claims skeptically and encourage them only as a way of appearing supportive and cajoling more admissions. Police tend to view the claims as a defense mechanism — a way for a suspect to admit guilt without having to recount the sordid details of the crime.

Morrissey testified that when Richard Lapointe said he was blacking something out, "I went along with the fact that he couldn't remember, and I said that ... it was important to remember. And I considered it as a defense mechanism on his part when he got to a sensitive area, and I would say, 'Why don't we start over?'"

But there is another explanation of why a suspect might say he was blacking out when confronted with false claims of overwhelming evidence against him.

An innocent person, believing that he somehow must be guilty, may seek to reconcile that belief with his lack of memory of the crime by concluding that he must have had a blackout.

Faced with false claims of strong evidence against him, "an innocent suspect, who naively assumes that police officers would not lie, is likely to experience confusion, anxiety, distress, and might ultimately come to doubt his or her memory," Ofshe wrote in a 1992 paper.

According to police testimony, Richard Lapointe made a number of claims about blacking out during the 9½ hours he was interrogated at the Manchester police station on July 4 and 5, 1989. Statements that he blacked out or couldn't remember some or all of the elements of the crime appear in all three of his written confessions.

Similarly, in Connecticut's notorious Peter Reilly case, Reilly repeatedly denied any memory of the murder of his mother, Barbara Gibbons, during eight hours of exhausting interrogation by the State Police the day after the murder.

He finally confessed only after being told he had failed a lie-detector test that could "read his brain," according to Donald S. Connery's account of the tape-recorded interrogation in the book *Guilty Until Proven Innocent.*

Connery said the police also told Reilly at least twice that his guilt could be proven through independent evidence — which was a lie.

A jury convicted Reilly of manslaughter, but eventually the charges against him were dismissed by a judge after the prosecutor died and his successor discovered that evidence of Reilly's innocence had been hidden.

The blackout issue also figured prominently in yet another interrogation in Florida — of Tom F. Sawyer, who confessed to the 1986 torture-murder of his next-door neighbor, Janet Staschek, in Clearwater.

Sawyer, a recovering alcoholic who hadn't had a drink in 13 months, confessed during 16 hours of police interrogation after he had worked a full day as a groundskeeper at a golf course.

Like Reilly, Sawyer confessed only after being told he had failed a lie-detector test, a questionable claim because of irregularities in the way the test was administered.

The detectives also falsely told Sawyer there was physical evidence of his guilt. They said his fingerprints had been found in the victim's apartment and car and that his hair samples matched hairs found on her body, according to Ofshe, who analyzed the tape-recorded interrogation and testified for Sawyer.

In excluding the confession, a Florida judge wrote that the interrogators undermined Sawyer's confidence in his memory by suggesting he could have had a blackout like those he had experienced when he was drinking.

The detectives also suggested that Sawyer's remorse might cause him to resume drinking if he failed to confess, according to the dismissal decision, which was upheld by a Florida appeals court.

In the face of those pressures, Sawyer's belief in his memory collapsed, and he agreed that he must have committed the crime, Ofshe wrote.

Richard Lapointe likewise was encouraged to believe that he might have blacked out a memory of murdering Bernice Martin.

Manchester police Detective Paul R. Lombardo testified that Lapointe asked him during the interrogation whether it might be possible for someone to commit a crime he couldn't remember. Lombardo said he replied it "might be possible."

Detective Morrissey admitted telling Karen Lapointe many things that were untrue, but he defended his statements to her that the police were trying to help her husband. "We were helping him to get to the truth," Morrissey testified.

Double Standard Unrealistic

In permitting police to use deception in the absence of a full video-tape recording of the interrogation, the courts would seem to believe that an interrogator can act like a scientist manipulating a sample on a laboratory slide. He is presumed able to dangle false information in front of a suspect but to observe and report the suspect's responses fairly and accurately.

But is that realistic in light of the officer's interest in solving the crime and the intense conflict of wills that can be involved in obtaining a confession from an unwilling suspect?

In addition, police deception involves a troubling moral ambiguity. The interrogator is licensed to ignore normal rules of decent human conduct by lying freely. But he then is expected to observe those rules scrupulously when reporting the interrogation and testifying in court.

Is it realistic to expect an officer to compartmentalize his behavior to that extent? Or is it more realistic to expect that the feeling of being above the rules that apply to others may seep into areas that are supposed to be sacrosanct, such as sworn testimony?

For Jerome H. Skolnick and Richard A. Leo, a law professor and graduate student at the University of California at Berkeley, the answers, respectively, are "no" and "yes."

"When courts allow police to deceive suspects for the good end of capturing criminals — even as, for example, in 'sting' operations — they may be tempted to be untruthful when offering testimony," the two wrote in a 1992 paper.

Another troubling aspect of police deception is that it is likely to be more effective against an innocent person or first-time offender than against a hardened criminal.

A repeat offender who has been lied to in past interrogations — and has had time to figure out what happened during his subsequent court case — is less likely to fall for police lies than a law-abiding person who naively trusts the police.

Deception Requires Safeguard

So what might be done to overcome the pitfalls of officially sanctioned police lying?

To take the position that police should never be allowed to lie would rule out all undercover investigations, which inevitably involve some deception.

But deception during an interrogation could be limited by requiring an officer to get advance approval from a supervisor for any specific tricks he planned to use. That might impress on police that deception is a sensitive technique and establish for the record that it had been used so it would he harder to deny and easier to identify any consequences that deviated from justice.

Morrissey testified that he got no approval from anyone before lying to Karen Lapointe.

In the end, police deception has the same effect as lying in any other human relationship: A person who lies is less likely to be believed. The police may undermine their credibility in the community when it becomes known they have lied.

To Skolnick and Leo, police deception is particularly corrosive in light of the deep division in attitudes between middle-class Americans and the urban poor.

Noting that "urban juries are increasingly composed of jurors disposed to be distrustful of police," they add:

"Deception by police during interrogation offers yet another reason for disbelieving law-enforcement witnesses when they take the stand, thus reducing police effectiveness as controllers of crime."

WITHOUT TAPE, CONFESSION CAN BE UNASSAILABLE

By ALEX WOOD

When there are serious disputes about what happened during police questioning that led a criminal suspect to sign a confession and there is no tape recording of the interrogation, the defense lawyer faces a dilemma from which there is virtually no escape.

On the one hand, he must convince a jury that his client is unreliable enough to have signed a false confession.

But he also must convince a jury that the defendant is reliable enough that his version of what happened during the questioning should be believed over that of a police officer.

When a confession-based case comes down to what lawyers call a "swearing contest" — the police officer's sworn testimony against that of a suspect who has signed a confession, sworn to it, and then sought to repudiate it — the officer is the obvious favorite to win.

But if the police tape the interrogation, clever psychologists and defense lawyers inevitably will pore over it word by word to find any slip-up that might persuade a judge to throw the confession out of court. Indeed, in suppressing confessions judges have been known to quote at length from transcripts of taped questioning, or even append the full text to their decisions, to support the conclusion that the confessions resulted from psychological manipulation and coercion.

In light of those circumstances, it is easy to see why police often choose not to tape their interrogations.

What is a good deal harder to understand is how that decision can be reconciled with the ultimate objective of the criminal justice system: to do justice.

It is a continuing source of puzzlement to some that the law and the courts in most states leave to police the decision about whether to tape interrogations.

Yale Kamisar, a University of Michigan law professor who has written extensively on criminal justice, says in one essay: "It is hard to see why the judges... are so apathetic about the apparent unwillingness of police interrogators to use tape recordings."

Kamisar's essay centers on an Iowa case involving the legal admissibility of a defendant's confession. The professor argues that one effect of recording would have been to save public money and judicial resources: "In all likelihood, the use of a recording device, a tiny administrative and financial burden, would have spared the state the need to contest the admissibility" of the defendant's "disclosures in five courts for eight years."

For Juries, A Clearer View

When a video recording is used in court, it can provide a jury with information available in virtually no other way.

The videotape of New York subway vigilante Bernhard Goetz's confession played a major role in his being acquitted of the major charges facing him, according to Professor George Dix of the University of Texas Law School.

The tape showed Goetz's "emotional explanation of the fear he had experienced before the incident and his prior victimization from assailants," Dix wrote in a 1989 article.

As a result, Dix wrote, the jury was undoubtedly convinced that Goetz shot four youths who had accosted him "in actual fear that they were about to assault and rob him."

The most common argument against taping confessions is that a guilty suspect may freeze up in the presence of a tape recorder or video camera and fail to confess.

"The only real reason advanced by police for their frequent failure to electronically record an entire interrogation is their claim that recordings tend to have a 'chilling effect' on a suspect's willingness to talk," the Alaska Supreme Court wrote in a 1985 decision.

The court rejected that argument on grounds that the accused has a constitutional right to remain silent, The court used the decision to require recording of all interrogations of suspects in Alaska police custody unless the police have a good excuse, such as an equipment failure.

Indeed, it is arguable that a visible tape recorder or camera does nothing more than remind the suspect of the familiar principle, "Anything you say can be used against you." And that's something the U.S. Supreme Court already requires police to tell suspects facing interrogation in police custody.

Moreover, the danger of inhibiting a suspect can be reduced or eliminated if the taping is covert. Easily hidden microphones, tape recorders, and even video cameras are widely available today.

The chief drawback to covert taping is similar to the problem with all police uses of deception: Ultimately, word of the practice will spread through the community, increasing suspicion and mistrust of the police.

Savvy repeat offenders will assume that their interrogations are being taped, while first-time offenders and the innocent may not.

Another argument against covert taping is that it eliminates an important check on the police. If a suspect knows he is being taped, it will be harder for a rogue police officer to conceal a tape from the courts.

Only three states — Alaska, Minnesota, and Texas [less completely] — require recording of interrogations of suspects in police custody. Britain also requires recording of most interrogations in police stations.

The possibility that police will lie about what happened during an interrogation is only one reason for requiring that it be recorded.

"Although there are undoubtedly cases where the testimony on one side or the other is intentionally false, dishonesty is not our main concern," the Alaska Supreme Court wrote. "Human memory is often faulty — people forget specific facts or reconstruct and interpret past events differently."

The court also stressed that it was not acting only to protect the accused:

> A recording also protects the public's interest in honest and effective law enforcement and the individual interests of those police officers wrongfully accused of improper tactics.
>
> A recording in many cases will aid law enforcement efforts, by confirming the content and the voluntariness of a confession when a defendant changes his testimony or claims falsely that his constitutional rights were violated.

One crucial issue with respect to recording is what is recorded. Many police departments turn on a tape recorder or video camera only at the end of the interrogation, asking the suspect to repeat admissions he already has made.

But by doing that the police still withhold crucial information, which taping of the complete interrogation would provide, about how the suspect was persuaded to make those admissions.

Though taping interrogations might mean more acquittals, it also could lead to more justice.

In upholding a trial judge's decision to throw out the confession of murder suspect Tom F. Sawyer, a Florida appellate court praised the Clearwater Police Department for its practice of tape-recording interrogations.

"We also recommend this practice to all other law enforcement agencies, so that challenges to future confessions can be exposed to the light of truth," the court wrote.

An article distributed by The Friends of Richard Lapointe, August 1995

HOW RICHARD LAPOINTE GOT HIS FRIENDS AND WHY HE NEEDS THEM

By ROBERT PERSKE

It all began on a bright spring day, May 6, 1992. I walked into Hartford Superior Courtroom A2 for the first time. I sat in the audience on the left side, behind the defendant, Richard Lapointe of Manchester, Connecticut, a 46-year-old, five-foot-four dishwasher with mental disabilities. I was there because a stranger called to say a travesty of justice was going on.

It was the first day of Lapointe's murder trial. I opened my notebook and prepared to jot down everything I saw and heard. Then it hit me that I was sitting on the left side of that courtroom alone. Everyone else sat on the right side, behind the prosecutor who was going for the death penalty.

Sitting in front of me was Lapointe, a soft, unathletic little man with an up-and-down thickness that even included his head. He wore thick glasses and hearing aids in both ears. It was easy to see how, when he grew up in Hartford's Charter Oaks Terrace housing project, he was given the nickname, "Mister Magoo."

All his life, he had fought valiantly to overcome the destructive effects of Dandy-Walker syndrome—a congenital brain malformation that caused a buildup of cerebrospinal fluid in his skull. Unfortunately, the condition was not diagnosed until age 15. By that time, the pressure had damaged many of his physical and mental functions: eyesight, hearing, stamina, muscle coordination, his ability to learn abstract concepts as well as sophisticated social skills. In his concrete way of thinking, he survived by pleasing the authority figures around him.

Even so, he married a young woman with cerebral palsy. They became the parents of a son they loved deeply. Lapointe was a good breadwinner for his family, doing what he did best, washing dishes. He was a faithful member of his local Catholic church and a regular member of the local Knights of Columbus.

Lapointe did have various odd habits due to his disability — staring at people too long, bringing up the same problem over and over again, and repeating the same corny jokes until the listener knew them by heart. But he was, above all, a family man with no criminal record and absolutely no history of violence. If anything, he would find a way to avoid any kind of confrontation. He had achieved a full life in the community in spite of his disabilities — until his life exploded on July 4, 1989.

On that holiday, Lapointe was helping his wife prepare for an evening picnic when the Manchester police called and asked if he would come to headquarters. He agreed to go and was driven to the station. As soon as he arrived, an officer read him the Miranda warning.

At that point, most people would become alarmed. But not Lapointe. He signed a statement that waived all of his rights. After all, why would he need to remain silent? Why would he need a lawyer?

He was walked past a number of "props" — large fake charts of supposed evidence and statements claiming that Lapointe was a brutal rapist and murderer. The police described the props in court as "devices for reducing the suspect's inhibitions for telling the truth." But because of Lapointe's eyesight and level of cognition, he didn't even react to them.

Next Lapointe was taken to an interrogation room where three detectives conducted a succession of unrecorded, one-on-one interrogations from 4:30 P.M. until 1:30 the next morning. The first detective told him that the police had massive amounts of evidence showing that he murdered his wife's grandmother, 88-year-old Bernice Martin, better than two years earlier on March 8, 1987.

Since Lapointe always took pains to befriend the police officers in town, he never dreamed that any of them would lie to him. Even so, he denied all accusations for quite some time.

Then, according to the detective's testimony, Lapointe gave his first "confession." The detective printed it out in large block letters:

"ON MARCH 8, 1987, I WAS RESPONSIBLE FOR BERNICE MARTIN'S DEATH AND IT WAS AN ACCI- DENT. MY MIND WENT BLANK."

That wasn't much of a confession for such an overpowering explosion of violence: raping with a blunt object, delivering ten stabs to the back and one to the abdomen, the restraining of wrists and the complicated fashioning of a strangulation "ligature" from strips of cloth — then setting fires in three separate locations within the apartment.

The second "confession" — different from the first — was typed. It contained 157 words and ended with, "If the evidence shows that I was there, and that I killed her, then I killed her. But I don't remember being there."

The third "confession" — different from the other two — was a 212-word statement that was again hand-printed by a detective. This one was more detailed, but it matched the police reports on the crime. During the trial, many forensic experts showed that the crime didn't happen the way the police reported it!

The police, now claiming to have their murderer, did a strange thing. Around 1:30 A.M. on July 5, they let him go home!

Unaware of his plight, Richard grabbed a few hours of sleep, woke up and walked two miles to his dishwashing job that began at 5:30 A.M. That evening, after a full day's work, he was arrested.

Bail was set for $500,000. His wife, who soon divorced him, and his eight-year-old son were pulled away by relatives who could not imagine that the police were mistaken. Lapointe awaited trial for nearly three years virtually without a visitor.

When the trial began, no person other than his public defenders appeared in court to support Lapointe. That first weekend, all I could think about was that small friendless man sitting all alone in that courtroom while the State of Connecticut went all out to kill him.

By 2:00 A.M. on Monday morning, my anguish peaked. I got out of bed and dialed into the answering machines of numerous persons who worked with people like Lapointe. In some instances I did more than share; I shouted.

Later, on Monday morning, eight people sat behind Lapointe. By the end of the 48-day trial, 40 new-found friends attended when they could. Every word of testimony and every legal argument took place with supporters sitting behind the little defendant.

Friends were there when the jurors, basing their decision mostly on the confessions (no physical evidence tied him directly to the crime), found Lapointe guilty.

Friends were there when the jury decided that Lapointe's disabilities were a mitigating factor and he should not be killed.

Friends were there when the judge sentenced Lapointe to "life without parole plus 60 years." And some of them wept.

The judge and lawyers went on to other cases, but we who chose to become Richard's friends have not gone away. We organized as The Friends of Richard Lapointe. We began meeting every other Wednesday evening in the community conference room of the Wethersfield, Connecticut, Burger King.

We are journalists, lawyers, psychologists, professors, detectives, nurses, teachers, court monitors, literacy volunteers, businessmen, state workers, citizen advocates, as well as numerous ordinary citizens whose sense of decency has been offended by what happened to Richard in a Connecticut court.

Today, there are better than 100 members who are on call or working in close-knit committees.

Since the trial, more than three years ago, I and the other Friends of Richard have tried the case over and over again in our minds and have asked numerous questions that are yet to be answered.

For example:

- If the officers thought they had the killer, why did they let him go home after the interrogation?
- Why didn't the judge suppress the three bizarre confessions? A retired chief of detectives who is a key member of our citizens' group has described Richard as a man who would have confessed to murdering Abraham Lincoln if the police had pressured him into saying so.

- Why didn't the detectives use recording devices during their interrogation of Richard as they did with others? There is no record — absolutely no record — of what went on during his interrogation.
- And most importantly, why can't the Manchester police department and the state's attorney do the honest and decent thing and admit they made a terrible mistake?

At any rate, The Friends of Richard Lapointe continue to thrive. But we have received numerous shots in the arm along the way:

- The Arc of Connecticut, an organization that is highly respected by the disability community, offered to back up Richard's friends with support services.
- Columnist and lawyer Tom Condon published "Reasonable Doubt," his 15-page investigative report that appeared in *The Hartford Courant's Northeast Magazine* on February 21, 1993. "Whoever raped and murdered Bernice Martin was a raging, violent maniac," Condon said. "Richard Lapointe is a meek and timid man who'd never struck his wife or child."
- Donald Connery, a former *Time-Life* foreign correspondent, was drawn into the case because of its similarities to Connecticut's famous Peter Reilly case of the 1970s. In his book *Guilty Until Proven Innocent*, he described how the teenager had been led by police interrogators to falsely confess to his mother's murder. Connery was so incensed by what had been done to Lapointe that he became a dynamic force in drawing legal and media attention to his plight.
- Playwright Arthur Miller, the major figure in winning Peter Reilly's freedom, agreed with Connery that this latest case was "worse than Reilly's." In an address to the Connecticut Bar Association in June of 1994, he said that both cases "rely basically on confessions brought about by very long interrogations, and not on evidence."
- On June 7, 1994, New Haven civil rights attorney John R. Williams and his associate, Norman Pattis, agreed to

represent Richard in an appeal before the state Supreme Court.

- *Washington Post* columnist Colman McCarthy traveled to Connecticut, visited with Richard in prison and interviewed individuals who had studied the case in detail. On September 6, 1994, he took the story to the nation via his syndicated column.
- On November 29, 1994, a Connecticut Public Television documentary, *A Passion for Justice*, centered on Richard's case. That documentary, by Ron Gould and Richard Furman, won an Emmy as "The best public affairs film in the New England region."
- The Connecticut chapter of the American Association on Mental Retardation, on December 15, 1994, presented its "Annual Award for Advocacy" to The Friends of Richard Lapointe.
- On January 9–13, 1995, staff writer Alex Wood published in the *Journal Inquirer* of Manchester a lengthy five-part analysis that exposed the police lies and deceits that led to Richard's arrest and prosecution.
- Six hard-hitting editorials have appeared in Connecticut's major newspapers, all claiming that what happened to Richard was unfair and unconstitutional.

The Friends of Richard can't prove it, but we believe that if our vulnerable little friend had been left all alone in that courtroom, he would have gotten the death penalty.

On the other hand, it hurts to think that he has now entered his seventh year of incarceration.

So we keep working.

PART II

"CONVICTING THE INNOCENT":

THE PUBLIC FORUM

AETNA HOME OFFICE AUDITORIUM, 9 AM TO 3 PM, HARTFORD, CONNECTICUT, SEPTEMBER 16, 1995

Taking a Stand

Margaret Dignoti

Good morning. I am Peg Dignoti, the Executive Director of The Arc of Connecticut (formerly the Connecticut Association for Retarded Citizens), and a charter member of The Friends of Richard Lapointe.

It is my pleasure this morning to welcome you on behalf of The Arc and The Friends of Richard Lapointe, which is a loosely knit, diverse group of citizens who are bound tightly together by a passionate desire to right a terrible wrong, to free Richard Lapointe and to prevent similar miscarriages of justice from happening in the future.

The Arc of Connecticut has long been concerned about the plight of people with mental disabilities caught up in the criminal justice system.

At the request — or maybe I should say *demand* — of Bob Perske, our staff started attending the trial of Richard Lapointe about three years ago. We were absolutely appalled at what we saw in the courtroom: a small, beleaguered, obviously disabled man who was clearly unaware of almost everything that was going on around him.

When the staff reported to our board about what was going on in court, the board voted to support Richard, and we kind of adopted The Friends of Richard. We gave them a home, or at least an office that they could work from — although their meetings continued to be held every other week at the Burger King community room in Wethersfield, to whom we are most grateful.

The Friends have worked incredibly hard putting together this

Margaret Dignoti, a staff member of Arc/CT since 1960 and its leader since 1981, is Connecticut's most admired and accomplished advocate of the civil and legal rights of persons with mental retardation.

forum. We hope today to educate ourselves to discover why
these tragic injustices occur, to
raise awareness of them, to learn
how we can help Richard better,
to find some solutions — some
ways to prevent similar miscarriages of justice from occurring
again.

We hope the day that we
have planned will be fast-paced
and thoughtful and thought-pro-
voking. We hope you will participate in the dialogue throughout
the day, and we also invite you
to be good to yourselves.

As a way of introducing Richard Lapointe today and more
broadly our topic, we would like

Margaret Dignoti.

to show you a clip from an Emmy award-winning documentary produced by Connecticut Public Television entitled *A Passion For Justice.*
As you watch this clip and throughout the day, please ask yourself
how you would feel if a member of your family confessed to a crime
that you know he or she did not commit, and if you then learned that
there was no audio or videotape or transcript of the nine-hour police
interrogation that led to the so-called confession, and there was no
lawyer present during the entire interrogation.

Richard Lapointe:
A Good Life Destroyed

Robert Perske, *Forum Co-Moderator*

These days, I am just a member of The Friends of Richard Lapointe because the case has attracted so many bright, hard-working, energizing people. I get put in my place quite often, and I'm proud to be in my place as just a good member of The Friends of Richard Lapointe.

I'm going to take a few minutes just to re-emphasize a few things about our friend, Richard.

I want you to picture a man who has a congenital brain malformation called Dandy-Walker. It's a terrible, damaging condition. Basically, it causes hydrocephalus that builds up fluid in the head and causes a lot of pressure. Today, luckily, it is diagnosed at birth and shunts and surgery take place and the pressure is off.

They didn't discover Rich's hydrocephalus until he was age fifteen, and by that time, the pressure had caused a lot of physical and mental damage.

He went through five brain surgeries to stop the damage from progressing. Today, at five foot four, he is the smallest member of the family. He needs hearing aids in both ears. He wears thick glasses.

He is not strong. A former employer had to let him go because he couldn't carry groceries to a car. He sometimes gets dizzy when he stops too fast, and I witnessed this once. He is concrete in thinking

ROBERT PERSKE, *a former president of Arc/CT and prolific author of such books as* Unequal Justice? *and the current* Deadly Innocence?, *has written extensively on the fate of crime suspects with mental disabilities. A work in progress is an in-depth account of the Lapointe injustice.*

and he doesn't abstract well. He called me not so long ago and said, "Hey, Bob, I wanted to call you this week but I couldn't because we were in lockdown. A guy got stabbed." I said, "Whoa! Somebody got stabbed. Where, Rich, where?" And he said, "On some guy's body."

He has a short attention span. He is an interesting little talker and he is full of corny jokes — jokes that we hear over and over again, and we have got them all memorized.

I asked him once if anybody had ever made him mad, and he responded by saying, "I just walk away." He says it's the better man

Robert Perske.

who can walk away. The point I want to get across is that Rich was a survivor in the community. In spite of everything, he was a valiant guy. He earned a living by doing the one thing he could do well, and that was washing dishes. He had enough good sense to know that if he didn't like this dishwashing job, he should get another dishwashing job before he left. That's better than some of us do, you know.

He married a young woman named Karen who had cerebral palsy. The couple had a son, Sean, whom he loved deeply and will continue to love as long as he lives. The family were active members of Saint Bridget's Church in Manchester, and they were at every church supper and church event they ever had. Sean attended Saint Bridget's School; Rich and Karen were good about looking after Sean and his education. Richard was a regular member of the Knights of Columbus, and he has never — repeat, never — shown physical violence to anyone.

It was corroborated that Richard never, ever, ever, even struck his wife or his child.

Well, that was Richard Lapointe until his life was exploded on July 4th, 1989, when the Manchester police asked him to come down and help them solve a crime. From 4:30 P.M. until 1:30 the next morning, they interrogated him. They got out of him three of the most bizarre confessions that I've ever heard in my life. They literally used the things he was good at surviving in the community on. They were using them against him in there. He relied on good authority figures for solving tough problems, and he saw them as good authority figures; he saw them as his friends. He tried to befriend all of the cops in Manchester. He was always trying to please persons in authority. His inability to abstract from concrete thought will show you right away that he never understood the Miranda reminder about his constitutional rights.

As far as he was concerned, waiving your rights meant that you wave to the right in the police station. You sure don't wave at the wrong.

His quickness for taking blame was because he figured if he took the blame they would like him more. Now let me repeat: *the police used those traits that helped him survive in the community to get a confession.* They could have taken those traits and got him to agree that he blew up the federal building in Oklahoma City.

After getting confessions that identified the monster of Manchester, the killer of an old lady, they let him go home. That's a puzzlement, and so is this: the Manchester police department has the latest high-tech recording equipment, and they used it. Yet they claimed to have no record of what went on between the police officers and Richard. All they had were three confessions that were printed or typed by the detectives and signed by Richard.

The confessions matched the police reports, not the forensic evidence. On the stand, the forensic evidence experts testified that the murderer who attacked Bernice Martin was like a raging, overpowering bull: stabbing her in the back ten times, stabbing her in the stomach once, raping her with a blunt object, masturbating on the bedclothes, binding her hands with strips of cloth, fashioning from strips of cloth a strangulation ligature so tight medical personnel had a heck of a hard time even taking it off, then setting fires in three places within the apartment to destroy the evidence. That was what the killer did. And that killer is still loose.

Well, folks, there's going to be other puzzlements we'll be talking about today. But I must tell you, I am appalled — I am utterly appalled that the State's Attorney, John Bailey, even brought the case.

We, The Friends of Richard, are ashamed for Judge David Barry because he refused to suppress three of the softest and strangest confessions I've ever read in my life, and I've read a great many — confessions that didn't match Richard, and certainly didn't match the crime. I feel a great sadness because most of Richard's in-laws believed the police reports right away. We are trained to believe whatever the police tell us, and I feel sad about that, but I guess I feel the deepest sadness for the criminal justice system where, sure, we are hard on crime, but being hard on crime doesn't mean smashing a vulnerable, innocent person.

I am puzzled because Richard never could have committed this crime. He is innocent, he is innocent, and yet the State of Connecticut laid it on him. And I wonder why it is that the State of Connecticut, the officials of the State of Connecticut, can't just do the honest thing and say they made a terrible mistake. All of us who are friends of Richard Lapointe know that he is innocent. *He is innocent.* He could not have done this crime. The timing was not there, nothing was there, and he deserves to be free.

Abuse of Power, Arrogance of Power

Donald Connery, *Forum Co-Moderator*

Good morning. My claim to fame these days is that I'm a student of Robert Perske and Peg Dignoti and their associates. I have learned a world of information during the last year and a half about mental retardation, about the workings of the brain, and all the related things that this case is about.

If it had not been for Bob Perske coming to Richard's rescue, none of us would be here; I wouldn't be here, and maybe I would be making money somewhere. But Bob is an inspiring figure. He is a one-man army out there, a kind of a Johnny Appleseed, who specializes — he is perhaps the only one in the country — in coming to the aid of individuals with mental impairments or learning disabilities who are caught up in the justice system.

Sometimes they are guilty and deserve punishment, but then they get screwed by the length of their sentences and by the difficulty of getting out of prison as soon as others.

And all too often they are innocent.

As for Peg Dignoti: she gave this citizens' group a home base. Her organization has nonprofit status. They have telephones. They have knowledge. I think it took great courage for this lady and her organization to commit themselves to what was, and still is, a highly controversial case.

Former Time-Life foreign correspondent DONALD CONNERY is the author of five books, including the definitive Reilly-case report, Guilty Until Proven Innocent. *He is currently investigating the 22-year wrongful imprisonment of Alabama's Michael Pardue.*

It *deserves* to be controversial.

In the last year and a half, some of us have succeeded in making it rather well known. My own ambition is to make Richard Lapointe what Peter Reilly was in the 1970s: the most famous innocent man in prison in the country. Why? So that everyone in the country will ask the powers that be in Connecticut: "What is this man doing in prison if he didn't commit the crime?"

Now, if you saw yesterday's *New York Times*, with Richard Lapointe's photograph, you will notice that the State's Attorney

Donald Connery.

in Hartford, James Thomas — who could have investigated this case once the alarm was sounded about a miscarriage of justice on his turf, who could have been a hero — Mr. Thomas says, "It's basically a *cause célèbre*. It represents the opinion of a select few that Mr. Lapointe is the so-called wrong man, but they are unable to point to anything substantive to indicate that he is, in fact, the wrong man."

Well, I love being a member of the elite few, although it's becoming the elite many.

Mr. Thomas forgets that most of the great advances in human civilization were made by individuals or an elite few. We have had some recent examples.

Think of Candy Lightner in California. Her daughter was killed by a drunk driver. She founded MADD, Mothers Against Drunk Driving, and within a few years brought about legislation in every state that has transformed the whole attitude of our courts and public about drunk driving offenses.

Think of Pamela Freyd. Her family was caught up in a false accusation of childhood sexual abuse a few years ago. She fought back by creating the False Memory Syndrome Foundation in Philadelphia. It began with a few families that had also been struck by the madness of "recovered memories" elicited from fragile patients by irresponsible therapists. She now has an organization providing information to some fifteen thousand families, and she has transformed national attitudes about that subject.

To me, Mr. Thomas' statement represents a cavalier attitude about citizen efforts in a democracy to correct something wrong, whether it is a miscarriage of justice or a faulty bridge over a river. People should be encouraged to speak out, not remain silent when they see a tragic mistake.

Let us be very clear about what is going on here. This case is about abuse of power and arrogance of power, and I take it personally. This is why I find myself involved in these judicial horror stories. I grew up in the 1930s. I was a child watching the rise of Hitler. I was sensitive to the fact that people were swept out of their homes by the Nazis. Later, as a foreign correspondent working in the Soviet Union, I knew about people who disappeared into psychiatric hospitals because of trumped-up accusations.

Whether it's a Holocaust covering millions of people — Jews, homosexuals, people with disabilities, people with incorrect opinions — or the millions who disappeared in the Soviet Union, it always comes down to one individual torn from his home, perhaps never to be seen again.

If you will read the information in your packets, Tom Condon's article and the others, you will see what happened, and what is happening, to one individual in the state of Connecticut — not years ago in some dark age but today, *right here and now.*

This man, Richard Lapointe, was essentially lured from his home, found to be (according to the police) a murderer — and then they let him go home, knowing full well he was not a murderer and no threat to his child, wife, neighbors, neighborhood. They let him go home because they knew he was not a killer, but they came for him the next day after figuring out how to concoct a bizarre police warrant, and they arrested him in 1989, and he disappeared into the prison system for two and a half years.

He was too poor to have an attorney. Most of the people in this room could call a lawyer. Lapointe didn't know any and he couldn't afford any. Two and a half years in Connecticut, the Constitution State, and he finally comes to trial. He is found guilty, and then he disappears into the prison system. The jury said, "Well, let's not kill him; we'll just put him away for life," and he would remain there forever if it were not for the citizens who have come to his rescue.

This whole business is appalling, and for a lot of reasons. I want to mention one of them by showing you a little wonder of technology. I have it in my pocket. It's smaller than a cigarette packet.

Behold! A tape recorder. And here's a tape, a mini-tape. Played at slow speed, you get two hours right here on this plastic bit the size of a pack of matches. Five of these little plastic things would give you the nine-hour Richard Lapointe interrogation, and we would know word-for-word who said what in that unforgivable interrogation.

But there was no taping of Lapointe's inquisition by the Manchester cops, at least nothing we know about: no audio, no video, no nothing. Yet in 1932, Yale professor Edwin Borchard wrote *Convicting The Innocent* – the title of our meeting today. In that work in 1932, all of sixty-three years ago, he recommended phonographic recordings of interrogations.

Professor Borchard provided documentation of 65 established cases of innocent persons erroneously convicted of major crimes. A very important and original book. Now the modern-day recorders of this phenomenon are Hugo Adam Bedau, Professor of Philosophy at Tufts, and Michael Radelet, a professor of sociology, assisted by Constance Putnam, a fine writer on social issues who also happens to be Mrs. Bedau.

Bedau and Radelet wrote the landmark November 1987 *Stanford Law Review* article about convicting the innocent. Then, just a few years ago, Bedau, Radelet and Putnam wrote *In Spite of Innocence*, now updated in a paperback edition. It is the Bible on this subject, and so it is my great honor to introduce Professor Bedau and Constance Putnam.

False Confessions and Other Follies

Hugo Adam Bedau & Constance Putnam

[PUTNAM:]

I confess. While we were working on *In Spite of Innocence*, my nephew came to visit us, and his visit precipitated something that helped me understand how important some of the cases in the book were.

My nephew at the time was in his mid-twenties. He was the manager in a small office, and he told us how one day that the police came, demanded to see Michael Putnam. When he identified himself, they took him into his office, shut the door and three of them sat down and grilled him for half an hour about some crime that had just taken place in the neighborhood. Michael knew nothing about it. He was completely innocent. It later turned out that the person who had committed the crime looked startlingly like Michael, but at the end of the half hour he was shaking from head to foot — this man is six-foot-four — and he said, "I was ready to tell them I did it. I was beside myself. I didn't know what to do."

That sort of set the stage, for me, for much of the work we were doing, because so many of these cases are cases of people who confess to crimes they didn't commit, and I think for most of us, it seems strange somebody would confess to something he had not done. Some

HUGO ADAM BEDAU is the Austin Fletcher Professor of Philosophy at Tufts University and editor of The Death Penalty in America. *He authored, with Professor Michael Radelet of the University of Florida, the landmark 1987* Stanford Law Review *article on miscarriages of justice in capital cases.* CONSTANCE PUTNAM, *a writer on a wide range of social issues, is the co-author (with Professors Bedau and Radelet) of* In Spite of Innocence: The Ordeal of 400 Americans Wrongly Convicted of Crimes Punishable By Death.

of the cases *are* very strange. I will share a couple of them, particularly strange ones, with you.

One took place in California in 1958. Robert Williams was convicted of first-degree murder and sentenced to life in prison. He had confessed to this crime because he was trying to impress his girlfriend. She hadn't been paying enough attention to him and he thought she might think he was a big macho type.

Unfortunately, the police believed him and, as I said, he was sentenced to life in prison.

Well, while he was in prison, he heard about another murder that had just been committed

Constance Putnam.

while he was in prison, and he thought the way to show the police that it was, in fact, possible to convict an innocent person, was to confess to this crime, too — which he obviously couldn't have committed because he was in prison.

Guess what? They believed him, a second time, and he was convicted of a second murder.

Well, lest you think that this is something that could happen only in flaky California, let me tell you about a case right here in Connecticut fifty years ago.

Delphine Bertrand was convicted of manslaughter after a guilty plea and sentenced to ten to fifteen years. In 1946, after the actual killers, two men, confessed, the indictment against Bertrand was dismissed and she was released. The two men were later convicted of the crime. They, and a third man, along with Bertrand, had visited the victim the night of the murder. Bertrand and the third man, however, were sexually intimate in another part of the house when the murder was taking place, and apparently, she thought it was better to be branded a killer than to reveal her sex life during the trial, so she voluntarily confessed to the crime.

Hugo Adam Bedau.

So people under duress may, indeed, do strange things. It may be a little difficult to put yourself in that position, but there you have two of the more bizarre examples of people who confessed to crimes they did not commit.

[BEDAU:]

As Constance pointed out from just these two cases, reality staggers our imagination. Nobody would think that either of the two cases that she has described really could happen, and yet they are among the four hundred and thirty cases that we tell about in our book, *In Spite Of Innocence.*

False confession, of course, is only one of several kinds of circumstances and causes which produce convictions of the innocent.

We have also nearly twenty cases not of false confessions, but of false guilty pleas, and as you may very well hear later, depending on which case Constance pulls out of the basket for you as we go on in this duet, when the defendant pleads guilty in court, the prosecution doesn't have to prove a thing. A home run the first time at bat.

The false confession, of course, can be used in evidence, and it is possible, as happens in most cases, that the defendant after a false confession then pleads not guilty, which poses some problems, but many other kinds of causes are involved in producing innocent people behind bars or even on Death Row. Among them are these:

- Negligent inquiry by the police not doing a thorough job.
- Overzealous pursuit and interpretation of slender evidence.
- Prosecutors who suppress exculpatory evidence and simply do not reveal it to the defense.

- Defense attorneys lacking the resources or the imagination to dig out evidence themselves.

One of the most important sources of error, of course, is mistaken eyewitness testimony. One of the most dramatic episodes we tell in our book is a Georgia case in which the defendant is sitting in the courtroom at one point in trial and on the witness stand is the wife of the victim. The prosecutor very carefully and conspicuously asks her whether she sees in the room the man who killed her husband, and she says, "Yes, I do, and there he is right over there" — but she was completely wrong, one hundred percent wrong. The man she identified was miles away at the time that that crime occurred, as was later clearly established, saving this man from the electric chair in Georgia.

But by far the strongest, most frequent cause of error in the cases that we have studied — and we have confined our research to actual or possible *capital* cases, we haven't talked in our research at all about cases of rape in non-capital jurisdictions or armed robbery or espionage or anything else, just murder and rape in jurisdictions where that crime was capital — by far, the most important and frequent cause is perjury, either suborned or voluntary by prosecution witnesses.

Misleading circumstantial evidence, classic source of error; incompetent defense counsel, you can always count on that; judicial refusal to permit into evidence exculpatory evidence; failure of the court and of the jury to consider adequately alibi evidence; completely mistaken theory of the cause of death; forensic testimony that was wrong.

One of our most dramatic instances is an Ohio case of a man who was innocent, yet sentenced to death, because the forensic expert interpreting the cause of death made a mistake, which was corrected several years later.

So that's the array of cases. Today, as you know, we are concentrating essentially only on one kind of error, the false confession. It divides in theory, *a priori*, into two subcategories: the coerced false confession and the voluntary false confession. Sometimes, as you will see from cases that Constance is about to put before you, it's very difficult to tell which is which.

[PUTNAM:]

One of the major reasons that people confess in some of these capital cases is their fear of the death penalty.

A troubling case in Ohio back in the seventies reminds us of Richard Lapointe. Jack Carmen was also somebody with obvious difficulty coping mentally; in fact, he was much more seriously incapacitated than Richard Lapointe. Despite that — or, indeed, perhaps *because* he was so compliant and so eager to please people and to cooperate — he was persuaded to confess to a grisly crime.

His court-appointed attorney, who was described by the prosecution as "active" and "experienced," arranged for Carmen to plead guilty to the murder charge. Later information indicated that fear of the death penalty had played a role in his client's decision. The death penalty had been reinstated in Ohio shortly before that.

It was clear that Carmen's IQ ranged somewhere between 43 and 55. Psychiatric testimony established that Carmen had an extremely faulty memory, could not always recognize his attorneys, asserted and then denied the very same things, and so on. His guilty plea was finally withdrawn and his conviction nullified, I'm happy to say.

A week before Christmas in 1977, a jury of five men and seven women voted to acquit Carmen of all charges. As Judge Fred J. Shoemaker read out the jury's verdict, the crowd in the courtroom burst into applause. Carmen's defense counsel, David Rebelin and Thomas Tyack, wept at the good news for their client.

When asked by reporters how he felt about his acquittal, Jack Carmen, ever eager to please and cooperate, said just, "I'm happy to be free again," adding, "I wish you guys a Merry Christmas."

Another case that is shocking in its — well, it's shocking in lots of ways. Fred Rogers, a church organist in southern California, nice young man — fairly simple young man, but nice young man — was convicted of murdering both his parents in a complicated case where it turned out later no murder had taken place at all; both were suicides. But Rogers said of his arrest,

> I was extremely frightened when they arrested me. I didn't know anything about the law or the way the courts worked. One of the officers told me they had enough evidence against

me to send me to the gas chamber. He told me that the only
way I could escape the death penalty was to sign a confession. He said that would make them go easy on me.

I will spare you all the details. He did confess as he was urged to
do. He then tried to plead not guilty by reason of insanity, but the
court and the jury would have none of it, and he was convicted and
sentenced to death. So much for outflanking the gas chamber by
confessing.

Later, on appeal, however, the court did not like the methods the
police had used to persuade young Rogers to confess. Furthermore, as
the court rightly noted, his confessions were of unusual importance
because of the lack of other evidence against him. Here again, you see
an echo of the Lapointe case. Judging the veracity of the confessions
was, of course, a matter for the jury rather than the appellate court,
but there were technical matters that enabled them to have the conviction overthrown.

A case in Illinois back in the fifties of Lloyd Miller is dramatic
also, because Miller was held without an opportunity to call his lawyer for many, many hours as he was interrogated. This is one of those
cases where it's not altogether clear how voluntary the confession he
finally signed was. He was desperate. He later retracted the confession. What's particularly dramatic about the Lloyd Miller case is that
he survived seven death sentences and death dates, including one less
than 74 hours from execution, but he finally was also shown to be
completely innocent. The entire evidence against him was his confession and fabricated evidence by the prosecution.

But lest you think all these cases go way back forty or fifty years,
let me share with you one from 1985:

Lavalle Burt, also in Illinois, convicted of murder. Conviction
was based on his confession, which he retracted two days after it was
given. He claimed he confessed because the police slapped him around,
told him he would be sentenced to death and not probation if he did
not confess, and said they had two eyewitnesses who incriminated
him. They failed to tell him he could have an attorney.

While sentencing was pending, the grandmother of the victim
contacted the judge and told him she had discovered a gun and that
she believed her daughter, not Burt, was the killer. Results of ballistics

tests on the weapon showed she was correct, and the judge vacated the conviction, happily.

[BEDAU:]

What you've just heard from Constance is a selection of four cases that we might say constitute the rational calculation of the defendant facing the choice, of the prosecution and of the court at a later juncture, between a death sentence and a long prison sentence. Under those circumstances, any one of us might very well plead guilty or give a false confession to save our lives.

The other kinds of cases that we are going to hear a few more examples of, however, don't constitute anything so clearly rational as the kinds of cases we have just described. They are far more disturbing — though what could be more disturbing than the Fred Rogers case, where he confesses under the pretext that that will avoid the death sentence or the gas chamber in California for him, only, in fact, that's exactly where he gets sentenced. What irony.

[PUTNAM:]

Three more cases, all from California. I think this is chance and not further evidence of how flaky Californians are.

These three cases might very well be called something like "unable to cope with the plight you're in."

Daniel Kamacho was convicted of first-degree murder and sentenced to life imprisonment, having been arrested and identified by an eyewitness. He confessed after admitting he had been high at the time of the murder. Only a little bit later, he remembered he wasn't high, he was in Mexico, but it looks as if he confessed largely because they had him there in the lineup. Fortunately, his alibi was verified and he was set free.

John Henry Fry, in the fifties, also in California, was convicted of manslaughter and sentenced to prison. It turned out he was so drunk at the time he was arrested that he had no idea what he was doing. He confessed, largely because he was completely drunk, and that later got straightened out as well.

More troubling, partly because it's more recent, in 1980 (though it took until '88 for this to get sorted out), was Jerry Bigelow in California, also convicted of first-degree murder. At Bigelow's retrial, the defense argued that the other chap had acted alone in the murder while Bigelow, intoxicated, slept in the back of the car. It turned out that several other people were able to testify that the other chap had boasted about the killing and the fact that he alone was responsible for it.

This, again, was somebody who confessed to something because he figured they had him caught and he didn't know any way out of it.

[BEDAU:]

That category of causation, if we may describe it that way, is not as infrequent as you might think, and again, if you can put yourself as an innocent person in the hands of the police under the circumstances that these defendants found themselves, you can imagine caving in, not knowing what kind of defense you should really give yourself.

You can't remember.

You were drunk.

Other kinds of circumstances intervened so that you can't give confidently a plausible alibi for yourself or some other account that would vindicate you and have the police release you.

And the deprivation of an attorney, the deprivation of sleep, these are factors that are going to propel you down the path of least resistance, which is to give the police what they want and what they are telling you to believe.

[PUTNAM:]

In 1959 in Florida, Joseph Shea was convicted of murder and sentenced to life. His conviction was based entirely on his false confession, which he later said he gave because he had suicidal urges and wanted to die in the electric chair.

In 1966, after an investigation led by Miami *Herald* reporter Gene Miller, Shea was retried and acquitted. A key to his acquittal was the admission by a police detective that he had denied Shea access to counsel and lied to him about having evidence against him in order to elicit the false confession.

In the U.S. Air Force at the time of the crime, Shea was dishonorably discharged and then spent six years in prison before being released. A Miami police officer commented that Shea was a neurotic of low intelligence who wanted to be punished. All of the evidence was against his being the killer, but the authorities just didn't want to know.

In 1967, Shea received an indemnification of forty-five thousand dollars from the state legislature, making him one of a very small handful of wrongfully convicted people who actually got some kind of indemnification.

In 1950 in Illinois, George Lettrich was convicted of killing a ten-year-old girl and sentenced to death. He confessed to the crime after being held incommunicado for sixty hours, but after the trial he repudiated his confession, claiming it had been extorted from him by third degree methods.

In 1952, the state supreme court said there was not a scintilla of evidence to connect Lettrich with that crime except his repudiated confession. And that the confession does not coincide with many of the known facts and cannot be entirely true. Again, we see the connection to the Lapointe case where the detailed confession doesn't jibe with the events.

[BEDAU:]
This category of case, depending upon how you view the facts, where there could either be a coerced and involuntary confession or a free confession voluntarily given, in a way poses the most troubling set of cases of them all.

If you think that the confession is unreliable, then you've got a basis for due process argument to throw it out, but if, in fact, it was given voluntarily, now the defense counsel has got a real problem.

We ask ourselves, why would anybody who is innocent ever confess to some horrible crime? That's the *obbligato* that runs through the background of this entire set of cases. Why would anybody who is really innocent ever confess to a crime?

Well, one answer is because they have been beaten up — and that's the last of the four kinds of cases that we are going to look at, and it's particularly relevant in the Lapointe case.

[PUTNAM:]
Melvin Beamon, Alabama, 1989. Beamon was convicted of a 1988 murder in Montgomery and sentenced to twenty-five years in prison.

After being arrested by police detectives, he was held 17 hours — he didn't know how lucky he was; at least it wasn't 60 hours — without being given access to an attorney or to a phone. While Beamon was in custody, the officers allegedly beat him, and at one point — get this for nice police conduct — threatened to shoot him if he did not confess. How many of you would refuse to confess at that point?

At trial, they gave false testimony against Beamon, as did other witnesses. Six weeks later, when an eyewitness to the crime exonerated Beamon, both the district attorney and Beamon's defense attorney asked the court to vacate the conviction. The request was granted and all charges were later dismissed.

When I come to something like that, I think to myself, Could *I* have held out? One of the most dramatic cases in the book is that of a young woman in Louisiana, Mary Kay Hampton. Again, someone of marginal mental capacities, age 16, extradited to Louisiana from the back hills of Kentucky — she had never been in Louisiana before — and told that if she didn't confess, she was going to "fry." She held out for forty-three days.

I submit that that young woman had more courage than most people I know. She finally pleaded guilty, and, as Hugo mentioned earlier, because she pleaded guilty without confessing, nobody ever had to prove anything. Fortunately, once again, the same newspaper man I mentioned a moment ago, Gene Miller, came to her rescue, as it were, and she ended up not spending a great deal of time in prison.

I want to mention one final case here, lest you think these are flaky California cases or Southern cases and we here in the Northeast don't need to worry about it.

This is Pennsylvania, 1976. Some of us don't think that was so long ago. A young white man, Robert Wilkinson, was convicted on five counts of murder in the firebombing of a home, but he was not formally sentenced because an appeal was immediately filed. An investigation by the Philadelphia *Inquirer* indicated that Wilkinson's confession had been coerced and at least seven other people had been beaten, threatened or otherwise coerced by the police into making false statements.

It's not enough to beat him so that he'll falsely confess; we'll beat a few other people so they incriminate him. One witness admitted he had lied at the trial, and another man confessed and pleaded guilty to the firebombing, for which two others were indicted.

The mildly retarded Wilkinson — do you hear another theme in here? People who simply aren't able to match their wits against the prosecutors — the mildly retarded Wilkinson was finally freed. He had spent fifteen months in prison. The convictions of several Philadelphia police officers for civil rights violations arising from their brutal and unlawful mistreatment — that's a quote from the official documents — of Wilkinson were sustained on appeal, and Wilkinson was later awarded damages of nearly a third of a million. Extremely unusual.

[BEDAU:]
I would like to turn our attention just a moment to two large issues that have not yet been addressed, except very indirectly, by the cases that we have presented to you so far.

The first question is: How do these mistakes, these catastrophic mistakes get discovered and corrected? And the second question is: Can mistakes of this sort, errors of this sort, be prevented in the future by new legislation?

As to the first, the short answer is, there is no uniform story to be told at all. I want to mention three different kinds of stories that help explain how these errors get caught and corrected.

One of them Constance just alluded to in mentioning the Shea case, and that is the role that is played by investigative journalists.

Gene Miller, a writer, now editor of the Miami *Herald*, played a really significant role in several different cases. Mary Kay Hampton in Louisiana owes her freedom in large part to the persistence of Gene Miller. Two black men who were on Death Row in Florida, Freddie Pitts and Wilbert Lee, owe their freedom to the resourceful investigation of the Miami *Herald*, conducted by Gene Miller. Miller is not alone, but he is perhaps America's preeminent journalist in making enormous contributions to freeing the innocent. Without that initiative, without that platform, who knows?

A second kind of source for the correction of these errors is organizations. Back in the 1950s, the famous mystery novelist, Erle Stanley Gardner, organized a group he called the Court of Last Resort. And if you do research in this general area — as Constance and our collaborator, Michael Radelet, and I have done — you will discover that the

Court of Last Resort managed to free a number of people, not just those on Death Row but others as well, who were innocent.

Today — and you will hear more about this later — we have an organization down in Princeton, New Jersey, known as Centurion Ministries doing the same kind of work. But these organizations are rare. They do not last forever. They are voluntary, not governmentally supported. The demands on their efforts far exceed their slender resources.

Occasionally, the judge or the prosecutor in the original case or the arresting officers will turn around and conclude that the person that they helped put in prison or on Death Row is, in fact, innocent, and there are some wonderful examples of officialdom playing a constructive role in identifying the wrongfully convicted and rescuing them from their fate.

But the fourth kind of story in this connection that I want to mention is particularly relevant to the Lapointe case, and that is the role that is played by people who aren't members of the family, who have no official position, have no access to the media as such, but are just decent citizens, like the people in this room — so many of them — who have devoted their care and attention to the Lapointe case.

There are three Connecticut cases in our catalog of four hundred twenty-three wrongful convictions in capital or capital-like cases, three cases from Connecticut. You've heard about two of them. You're going to hear more about the Peter Reilly case. Constance read you the story of Delphine Bertrand, but there is another case that you probably don't know about. It's the case of Luigi Lanzillo. Let me read you about that.

Lanzillo was convicted of second-degree murder and sentenced to life imprisonment in Connecticut. He was implicated when a gun found at the murder scene was identified as his. His brother, Carmello, had taken it without Luigi's knowledge. Luigi and two others were convicted of the crime, and all were sentenced to death and executed in 1918.

A confession from the condemned men written just before their execution absolved Luigi Lanzillo of any participation in the crime. Not until ten years later, however, after sustained pleas from concerned citizens, like people in this room, including attorneys for two of the three men executed for the crime, was Lanzillo pardoned and released.

So there's precedent right here in Connecticut for the kind of work that you are doing on the Lapointe case, and don't underestimate the extent to which you can produce good effects.

Let me turn to the second question I mentioned: Can these kinds of mistakes be prevented in the future?

You're going to hear more about the possible statutory requirement that some states already have but that Connecticut and, so far as I know, Massachusetts, where we live, do not have, and that is the requirement that if police are going to use a confession at a trial against the defendant, they have to produce a tape recording of the conditions in which that confession was given.

That is a possible remedy. I'm sure that it would help if such laws were required, but since so many of the causes, as you have seen from what I said earlier, that account for these errors have the character that they do, I'm afraid we are stuck with the risk of convicting and perhaps executing the innocent from here on out.

To cite but one example, there's no way in which we can enact and enforce a law to keep a witness from making a good-faith error, such as the lady who identified the killer of her husband in that Georgia courtroom. That was a good-faith error. There's no law that can prevent that, nor is there any law that can prevent bad-faith error, perjured testimony, but these are the kinds of principal causes that account for innocent people being behind bars today and yesterday.

I think it's foolish to hope that even if the bar association, the courts and prosecutors were able to agree — which, of course, they aren't — on how reform should be instituted, that we could see a significant reduction in the likelihood of these cases, especially in the most serious instances.

[PUTNAM:]

I want to end with one more case that again has some troubling parallels to the Lapointe case. It is the case of Melvin Reynolds in Missouri. It has some troubling overlap with another Missouri case, that of Johnny Lee Wilson, that you will also hear about later today.

This was a crime where there was both sexual abuse and murder — in this case, not an 88-year-old woman but a 4-year-old boy. If there is anything that upsets the populace more than the murder and rape of an elderly woman, it is murder and rape of a small child.

Suspicion fell on Melvin Reynolds, twenty-five, one of the many who had joined in the search for the boy's killer. An anonymous tip had informed the police that Reynolds had been seen at the mall on the day of the murder in Eric's company. When the police asked Reynolds to confirm this tip, he had first denied it and then said, well, yes, he had been at the mall.

That was all the police needed to take him in for a polygraph test. Terribly agitated, Reynolds spent four hours on the lie detector. Even so, the results strongly indicated he was not the man the police were looking for, and so they released him. They were not through, however, and they discovered he had suffered sexual abuse himself as a child, and they got a rumor, which turned out later to be completely false, that he had once sexually abused his 3-year-old nephew. That was enough. They hauled him in again.

In December, they arranged to give him sodium amitol, a so-called truth serum injection. Through all this investigation, not to say harassment — I'm skipping some of the details — Reynolds obliged the police at every turn. He never had the assistance he desperately needed of a lawyer to help him protect his rights. Then, under the truth serum, he let slip the words, "before I killed — before I went to the unemployment office..." This convinced the police they should keep him under surveillance.

Two months later, they brought him in again for yet another round of questioning. Still cooperative, this time he spent fourteen hours in the basement of the police headquarters, as he was grilled anew.

The police accused him of various thefts and told him if he went to jail, he would never be married. He had just gotten engaged. But they were willing to suspend further charges for the petty larcenies, they said, provided he would help them solve the murder. The scene in the police basement, as Terry Gainey describes it in his book *St. Joseph's Children*, was pathetic. After denying once again that he had killed the boy, Reynolds finally looked up at his interrogator — and I'm quoting now from Gainey's book — "appeasingly, like a dog with his ears pressed back against his head and said, 'I'll say so if you want me to.'"

To be sure, this was not a very convincing confession, but it was better than nothing. Once they made this breakthrough in Reynolds' resistance, the police were able to persuade the hapless young man to embellish his confession with enough details to warrant their arresting him.

[BEDAU:]

We have tried to give you in this half-hour a sketch of the kind of material you can find in greater detail and with greater variety in the *Stanford Law Review* article of 1987 and the book *In Spite Of Innocence* of 1992 and the new paperback edition of 1993-1994, and we hope hereby to have helped set the stage for the rest of today's proceeding.

When Will It Ever End?

Peter Reilly

Good morning. My name is Peter Reilly. [Audience stands, applauds.]
Thank you very much.

It's been twenty-two years since the death of my mother, Barbara
Gibbons. Not a day has passed that I haven't thought of her. Few
people, if any, could have known her as I did: a pioneer raising a
child alone, all the sacrificing so that I could have the things I needed,
never getting upset if I didn't get the best grades, but being sure I
knew that it was very important to give everything my very best effort
and to complete the things that I do — and I guess that's what I'm
doing here today, attempting to complete something that began so
many years ago.

This is why the Richard Lapointe case strikes so close to home. I
see the same things happening here that happened to me.

I see a cycle occurring, a cycle that must stop. This appears to be
the importance of getting a confession from a suspect and hanging
the entire case on that confession.

I understand the true importance of a confession, but when there
is no physical evidence, or the physical evidence doesn't confirm the
confession, *there is a problem*. That problem seems to be overlooked
time and time again.

There also is a practice of trimming, manipulating and squeezing
that evidence so that it will appear to be something other than what it
is. In some cases, just not using it because it doesn't fit the picture.
How easily exculpatory evidence can be lost or misfiled.

Cases in point [in Connecticut]: *State vs. Harold Israel*, 1924; *State
vs. Harry Solberg*, 1966 [told in Mildred Savage's *A Great Fall*]; *State vs.
Peter Reilly*, 1973; and now, *State vs. Richard Lapointe*.

Will these practices ever end?

Alone. I was 18 years old when I experienced this sitting in a cell in the Litchfield correctional center, reading *The Defense Never Rests* by F. Lee Bailey, a retired Marine Corps pilot and a world-renowned defense attorney.

He said this about being alone:

> If I ran a school for criminal lawyers, I would teach them all to fly. I would send them up when the weather was rough, when the planes were in tough shape, when the birds were walking. The ones who survived would understand the meaning of *alone*.

For a brief moment, I could understand exactly what he was talking about: To be kept awake for many hours, fatigued, shocked that your only family was gone, in a strange and imposing place surrounded by police who continued to tell you that you must have done this horrible thing and that nobody cares or has asked about you — under these conditions, you would say and sign anything they wanted.

The psychological games that are played during an interrogation such as this are difficult at best to understand: assured by authorities you don't remember things, being led to doubt your own memory, having things suggested to you only to have those things pop up in a conversation a short time later but from your own lips.

It is only by the examination of recordings of these interrogations that one can truly understand what goes on behind the closed doors.

This activity in and of itself is evidence — evidence that the jury could and should hear. It is evidence that Richard Lapointe's jury never had the opportunity to hear.

Why were there no recordings made of this interrogation? Should police be able to record or not record interrogations at their discretion? This is too powerful a tool to be left in the hands of police without some rules of law.

PETER REILLY, now a 40-year-old musician, was the focus of America's most publicized "wrong-man" case in the early 1970s when he was convicted of his mother's murder and later rescued by citizen action, press exposures and court rulings..

Approximately a week ago while viewing CNN, I observed a five-year-old boy conduct an interview with the President of the United States. He recorded that interview with a Fisher-Price tape recorder. I was appalled that a child could tape-record the President of the United States but a professional police department could fail to record the interrogation of Richard Lapointe.

We, the law-abiding, taxpaying citizens of Connecticut, the Constitution State, should demand that it become law that all interrogations conducted by police departments in the state of Connecticut must be audio- and video-recorded.

There was a time when one never questioned the integrity of a police officer or a state's attorney. Those times are long gone. It was a fairy tale told to us as children, but we have grown up. It is in a time when we hear of the attack on Randy Weaver's family by the FBI, the resignation of Senator Packwood and the blatant perjury of Mark Fuhrman. It is only reasonable that we make these requests.

Thank you.

At this time, I would like to introduce my friend, an individual without whose help I might have spent the better part of the last twenty years in a jail cell, Mr. Arthur Miller.

Even Galileo Confessed

Arthur Miller

What I have to say on the issues of the Lapointe fiasco doesn't require a long, elaborate speech. I'm not an expert on crime or the law, but over the years, I have given a good deal of thought to the business of confessions, in my life as well as my plays.

Perhaps I could throw some little light on this very complex process in human psychology.

The British system is not, in every respect, a model for others to follow, but in one respect it ought to be an example.

In an interrogation of a person like Lapointe, the presence of a neutral aide would be required during an interrogation by police to ensure that the accused understands what the questions put to him really mean, what he is admitting to, if he admits to anything, what his legal rights are, and so forth.

The assumption is that there are malleable people who will reach to confession in order to relieve themselves, even momentarily, of the pressures of interrogation by authority figures.

Quite probably, most people when confronted by authority have, to some degree, a tendency to want to placate them so as to gain their approbation, but there are people so psychologically dependent as to leave them defenseless to one or another degree before the demands of authority. For this reason alone, a verdict in a capital crime cannot, it seems to me, rely solely or even mainly upon confession as a primary support.

ARTHUR MILLER, world-renowned playwright, Pulitzer Prize-winner and creator of such works as Death of a Salesman *and* The Crucible, *was the primary force in recruiting media and professional help to overturn the Reilly injustice.*

Arthur
Miller and
Peter
Reilly.

The record of mankind is full of confessions of events that either never happened or to which the accused has little or no connection. After all, even Galileo confessed that the sun and all the stars revolved around the motionless earth rather than face the wrath of the church.

Confronted with great power, against which one has only a fragile defense, confession can begin to look like a door to freedom.

Confession can very readily turn into a kind of coin with which to buy one's way out of a frightening and painful situation.

How then are we to indict the criminal? Is there a good substitute for confession as the mainstay of the prosecution's case?

For starters, I would suggest *evidence*.

There is a long and tragic history behind the undue reliance upon confession by prosecutors. A play of mine, *The Crucible*, is presently being made into a film in Massachusetts. If you have seen or read it, you know that the whole disaster which descended on Salem, Massachusetts, in 1692 sprang from the idea that the state could rightfully require confessions of people accused of having practiced witchcraft — and, faced with resistance by those who denied the charge, the court soon allowed what was called *spectral evidence*.

This consisted of claims by mainly teenage girls of being afflicted by the spirits of the accused, spirits which tortured and terrified them, in order to get them to join the devil in his plot to overthrow Christian civilization.

Simple as that. You either confess that you had, indeed, sent out your spirit to torture one of the girls into obeying the devil, or, if you refuse confession, you hang. Since evidence was spectral — invisible, undetectable, excepting by the accusers — evidence and accusation became one and the same thing.

And so confession quickly rose to become queen of the whole misbegotten procedure, veritable monarch of that court.

Naturally, given the threat of hanging, there were an awful lot of confessors, but some brave souls refused on principle to pretend to confess their non-existent guilt and twenty-one of them were, indeed, hanged.

The whole thing was only stopped by public revulsion when some very reputable people went to their deaths and when it was finally obvious that no one was really safe. But this kind of refusal took a lot of character when the combined power of both state and your own church were drawn up against you. It was a theocracy, in effect, a combination of church and state — the kind of regime, incidentally, which some Americans are yearning for again.

If one steps back and looks at this absolute reliance on confession from a world perspective, a certain equation emerges; namely, that the less evidence you have, the more vital the confession becomes for your case.

Bureaucracies love confessions because they are so persuasive. After all, the man admitted himself that he did it. What could be more conclusive? Would you ever admit to something you hadn't done? Of course not. But, of course, with a limited ability to understand your situation or a limited self-regard, you just might, and there are other circumstances when a confession might be quite sensible, no matter how innocent you might be.

A few years back, I was in my Grove Press publisher's office when a lady entered, a Chinese woman named Nien Cheng, who had recently published a remarkable memoir called "Life And Death In Shanghai." Nien Cheng had spent six years in a Chinese prison, four of them in solitary confinement, and in her final year to humiliate her further, they bound her hands behind her back with wire, forcing her to eat like an animal.

As the well-to-do widow of an executive of Standard Oil in China, who worse yet was fluent in English, it was logical to accuse her of harboring anti-Communist ideas and of spying for America.

When she refused to confess to these charges, she was jailed.

After half a decade had passed and the Cultural Revolution had blown itself out and the ruling Gang Of Four brought down, the warden of the prison walked into her cell and happily told her she could go now, she was free. She refused to leave her cell until she had a letter from the government stating she was an innocent person who had been imprisoned without cause and had simply refused to confess to a crime she had not committed. It took some months, but she finally got that letter.

She seemed very moved to meet me, and I did not understand why, in fact. I thought I saw tears in her eyes when she heard my name. She explained her feelings. Once freed, a good friend, a theater director, insisted that she see a show put on called *The Crucible.*

"I had been told it was written by an American," she told me, "but as I heard the dialogue, I assumed that the director had rewritten the dialogue for a Chinese audience, because the questions asked of the accused — the threatening demand for confession — was exactly the same as the questions I had been asked by the Cultural Revolutionaries."

How could an American have known this? I told her that these questions were all taken out of the record of the 1692 Salem witchcraft trials, and also were the same as the questions asked by Joe McCarthy and the House Committee On Un-American Activities, and that if there were ever to be a cure for this confession hunger, it can only be a reliance upon *evidence*, evidence of criminal actions — the last thing in the world that McCarthy, the House Committee On Un-American Activities, or the Chinese Revolutionaries were interested in looking for.

After the Reilly case demonstrated that a confession can, in fact, be pressed out of a completely innocent person, one would have thought that we in Connecticut would have done with this kind of abuse. Two or three reporters have called me about this forum, asking me why I was involving myself in it.

Of course, if it could happen to Reilly and Lapointe, it could happen to me, but that selfish answer is really not the whole of it. Justice is, after all, the noblest attribute of a civilization, and injustice the most noxious charge that can be made against it.

But I have an ulterior and unmentionable motive, too, for being here. I would like to protect the police, even from themselves. We need them. We need their principled upholding of the law, and possibly the quickest and easiest way of protecting the police is to require that interrogations be recorded, even videotaped, so that a disinterested observer can know what actually transpired.

The interrogation of Lapointe, incredibly enough, has no record. At least in the Reilly case, one could read in the recorded interrogation that after Peter had kept repeating that he had no memory of having attacked his mother, the police interrogator happily assured the boy that in fact he most likely would have wiped out the memory if he had done it, but remembering it or not, it was perfectly all right to confess to killing her anyway.

There, we had a record of the absurdity. Here, we can only look to the absence of hard evidence that Lapointe is indeed a murderer, but my point is that confession can easily become the way out, the way back to peace and quiet and reality, even if only to be enjoyed in a jail cell.

Clearly, a re-examination of the case against Lapointe is imperative, but, of course, something more than Lapointe's fate is at stake here.

In the final analysis, the question is whether the real murderer is out there still and is capable of striking again.

QUESTION TIME

NAT LAURENDI, a retired detective of the New York City Police Department, tells of "having been involved in many celebrated cases in New York where false confessions were an issue." He asks Peter Reilly about the sentiment of the Connecticut State Police toward him since he was exonerated.

REILLY: They don't approach me directly. They did say in the press, when it was the twenty-year anniversary of the death of my mother, her murder — they basically said that they stood by their original investigation, and they just don't seem to want to change their minds.

LAURENDI: Correct. They still feel you did it and you got away with murder; is that true?

REILLY: That appears to be their opinion, unfortunately.

LAURENDI: Law enforcement people — and I know because I've been one for 25 years — will never change their minds. Neither will prosecutors. They build up their resources; they have to fight the oncoming enemy; this is a pattern throughout the United States. Police and prosecutors and judges will never change their minds once a person has been convicted and given justice, a fair trial.

You must have a movement, just like Peter had with Mr. Miller and others. You must have a force to push behind you, to let the courts know. Somebody has to make a move; otherwise it just goes on, these miscarriages of justice.

DONALD CONNERY: About the Reilly case, let me add that the standard line from the State Police, as part of a deliberately created legend that says they did no wrong, is to tell inquiring journalists that Peter was, is and always will be guilty in their eyes. Except that they put it in convoluted language, not using his name. This is an exact quote from one newspaper: "Our position is that we caught the killer and that he was found guilty in a court of law. The subsequent reinvestigation [which, in fact, brought further disgrace on the department] did nothing to change that fact as far as we're concerned."

ARTHUR MILLER: There is one exception to what you're saying, and that is that the former State Police commander, Cleveland Fuessenich, did personally apologize to Peter for the whole thing, after he retired.

CONNERY: Yes, he was one of the truly honorable officials in that wretched case. He was the commissioner at the time Peter's mother was murdered. Later on, when I went to him and asked him to look at the transcript of Peter's interrogation, he was man enough to say that a terrible thing had been done to Peter. He helped me a great deal as I looked into the reasons for the wrongful conviction, and he was very public in accepting responsibility for it — for not more closely supervising the rogue detective who conducted the investigation.

LAURENDI: Could I ask Peter another question? The Miranda warning was in effect at the time of your alleged crime. Did you have an attorney there?

REILLY: Yes, I was advised of my Miranda rights, but to tell you truthfully, absolutely truthfully, my state of mind was that I hadn't done anything wrong and I felt that only a criminal really needed an attorney, and this was all going to come out in the wash.

LAURENDI: As a polygraphist working for criminal defense lawyers, I get cases where a person has confessed to police and now recants. Some of them confess after a polygraph test; some of them are false confessions; and after I had testified in New York state, charges were dropped in two or three cases; two of them went to trial, they were acquitted; so people still do confess notwithstanding the Miranda warning. They don't know what it's all about, so the question raised from people in law enforcement, detectives and prosecutors, is this: Why would somebody confess if he didn't do it? That is the burning question.

REILLY: I was so tired and so confused and so fatigued from this ordeal, my only family dead, the only people I knew, told by the police that my friends, or I thought my friends, weren't interested, nobody was asking for me. At that point, I would have signed anything. Anything they wanted me to sign, I would have signed.

LAURA KLEINMAN: I'm an employee of the State of Connecticut, Department of Mental Retardation. I work with people who are similar to Richard. They live out in the community in their own apartments.

I'm curious as to what advice you would give us. We teach them that the police are their friends. What advice would you give us if they are brought in, asked friendly questions, et cetera? What should we teach them to say, or to avoid?

REILLY: They have the same rights that you and I have. They have the Miranda rights. Teach them the Miranda rights. Teach them there's no reason to be afraid to say, "I would like to have an attorney."

I might say to attorneys out there, *please take the time to speak with your clients* — people buying houses, whatever the legal matter may be. Ask them to bring the children and let the children meet you. Don't be a larger-than-life individual in the eyes of these children. Let them know there's somebody out there that Mom and Dad say is okay to call in times of emergency or trouble.

"I'm Guilty If You Say So"

Richard Ofshe

It's always a bit depressing when you plan to speak about something and you hear far more articulate people say much of what you had planned to talk about, so you look at your notes and you say, *What will I do now?* So I find myself in that position, and bear with me.

There are one or two things I perhaps should say.

Over the last few hours, the focus of this meeting has started talking about cases in which people have been found guilty of crimes they did not commit, and with Peter Reilly's speaking, we have begun to see that the light needs to shift, because the issue is not an issue of the people who confess. It is an issue about *the police who make them confess.*

I see interrogations from all over the country. I review interrogations that lead to non-coerced, reliable confessions of crimes undoubtedly committed by the people who are confessing — and I see confessions on which people are sometimes convicted of crimes that there is no way on God's earth they could have committed.

If I took ten of those transcripts and I handed them to anyone in this room and said, sort these into two piles, five true confessions, five false confessions, I submit everyone could do it and could do it accurately.

The difference between a true and a false confession is glaringly

RICHARD OFSHE, *Professor of Social Psychology at the University of California, Berkeley, won the 1979 Pulitzer Prize for exposing the Syanon cult. He is the nation's top expert on psychological coercion leading to wrongful convictions. Co-author of* Making Monsters: False Memories, Psychotherapy, and Sexual Hysteria, *he is now writing a book on false confessions.*

obvious when you see them side by side. A false confession is the product of police incompetence, the product of police viciousness, the product of the political necessity to close a case. It is nothing less than that.

Sometimes the incompetence is not intended. Sometimes interrogators elicit false confessions using techniques that they shouldn't have used, but that police all over the country use, and they simply do not know what they are doing. They have not been trained to detect false confession.

I don't believe that, in most of the cases I look at, the officers *want* to produce a false confession. They manage to keep themselves believing that the person who has confessed actually committed the crime — despite the fact that, looked at dispassionately, one has to wonder how anyone could support that belief in the face of the disconfirmations. But the passion, the pursuit, the desire to finish the case that takes over interrogators when they interrogate blinds them to what they are doing in some cases, and they blunder into making a horrible mistake that they did not want to make and they will never admit that they made once it's over.

In other cases, it's hard to conclude anything other than that the police simply don't care. They simply are seeking to get a confession, to close a case that is causing them a problem.

In my experience, the kinds of egregious false confessions that I see come about in cases that are high-profile. They are cases in which the community is outraged, the crime is heinous, the police are under enormous pressure. They have to solve the crime, and in all likelihood, they will never be able to do it, because in all likelihood, in precisely this kind of crime, the person responsible does not know the victim, may not even be a member of the community. It is someone who will come and commit the crime and then disappear, and that person will never be found through the methods of Sherlock Holmes. That person is likely to be found only by accident.

Under those circumstances, the police will not be able to satisfy the political demand that the crime be solved, so what they do is turn to the statistically most likely suspects — and people will say the most likely person to kill an individual is the spouse or someone who knows the person. And statistically, that may be true, but that's a misuse of statistics.

Not all spouses are likely to commit murder. It's usually the case that if a spouse commits murder, the marriage was not ideal. We don't kill our friends willy-nilly just because we know them. The statistical category that you're more likely to be the killer if you know the person is true, but trivial — but often, police will simply ignore what they should pay attention to and capitalize on this police wisdom and bring in someone like Richard Lapointe to be interrogated.

Richard Ofshe.

Because the only way they will solve the crime is through producing a confession in response to interrogation, and it's no accident that the interrogations I review when they are recorded are often almost interchangeable from one region of the country to another, from one police agency to another, from one point in time to another — because the folklore of interrogation has been known since the Inquisition. It was known in Salem and it's known today, and it is taught to police in in-service training courses. They are trained to do it and it's all very simple.

When looked at from a distance, it's perfectly obvious what is happening. When trapped inside an investigation, it is overwhelming, it is confusing and it is powerful.

There is one statistic we have on this, and it's based on a single case, but it is the only statistic we have. If one generalizes from that, one has to presume that the probability is about point six that someone randomly selected, exposed to an unrestrained police interrogation, will give a confession to a crime he did not commit. I take that number from the Phoenix Temple murder case.

In my judgment, this is one of the most important confession cases of the 20th century, a case in which every kind of confession is illustrated — a case in which nine Buddhists were murdered at a temple outside of Phoenix. It created international attention. The Thai ambassador was flying in and out of Phoenix because the victims were Thai Buddhists: six monks, a nun and two people affiliated with the temple, killed execution style. The pressure on the police was enormous. They *had* to solve this crime.

The 75-person task force put together to solve it was sitting around twiddling their collective thumbs because they had no idea what to do when they received a phone call from a man named Mike McGraw. McGraw exemplifies the one kind of confession that is attributable to a defect in the individual who gave it. It's called a *voluntary false confession*. It's voluntary because the police are not involved in it. The decision to confess and the confession itself are given without police influence.

Mike McGraw picked up the phone, called the Phoenix sheriff's department, and confessed to participation in the Phoenix Temple murder massacre. He called from a psychiatric hospital in Tucson. Nothing could be more classic.

Ordinarily, police are accustomed to getting voluntary false confessions from people like Mike McGraw or from people who are, perhaps not in a mental institution, but are nevertheless seeking attention. They know that this is likely to happen, and it is likely to be a great waste of their time, so they do the very sensible thing. When someone calls up to confess, they require that the person prove that he committed the crime. Tell me something about it that only the killer could know; otherwise, get out of my face, leave me alone, don't waste my time. But because the Phoenix police — the sheriff's department — was desperate, they didn't bother to do that. Instead, they went down to Tucson, got McGraw out of the hospital, brought him to Phoenix and interrogated him. It's on tape and I have the transcript. He knew nothing about the crime.

And as the officers became angry with McGraw, they threatened him. They told him you better tell us who else was involved, because if you don't, you're in trouble; if you tell us who else was involved, we'll check it out, and if it proves to be nothing, we'll take you back to the hospital.

Under these conditions, McGraw named five people that he knew from Tucson. They did not necessarily know one another. They ranged from a junior college student to one man with a prior burglary conviction, and they were young in the main.

The police went down to Tucson, grabbed the five of them, hauled them back to Phoenix and interrogated all five of them on tape, interchangeable interrogation teams.

These five men were quasi-randomly selected. *Three of the five of them gave false confessions to mass murder* — and we know that they were false confessions because a few weeks later, the *real* killers were caught. In fact, the police already had in their possession the murder weapon. It was a Marlin .22 rifle. They had been confiscating them. They got some information from a military police officer who was on guard at the gate to the local Air Force base when these two adolescents came through the gate. He noticed a well-worn-looking beat-up Marlin .22 rifle on the back seat of the car. That was on the morning following the night of the executions. He made a report of it, and that report got to the Phoenix sheriff's department, and they went out and confiscated the rifle for ballistics testing. They couldn't get a straight answer from the kid they got it from as to why he had it that night and what was going on. It was enough that under ordinary circumstances would have nominated that young man as a suspect. But they just took the rifle, and because the call from Mike McGraw came in that night, they forgot about it. It sat in a corner of an office for five weeks before anyone remembered to send it down for a ballistics check.

In the interim, they got confessions from the men from Tucson; they were arrested; the case was proclaimed as solved; the sheriff had a press conference, took credit for it, probably was thinking about running for governor. Then, five weeks later, the real killers were identified. Search warrants were gotten; loot from the robbery was found in their homes. Two young men, Jonathan Doody and Alex Garcia, had committed the crimes.

Doody and Garcia were brought down for interrogation. Their interrogations were tape-recorded, and in their interrogations — which were coercive, which never would have held up in court had they been required to — one of the truly frightening things about the Phoenix Temple case expresses itself. Desperate to prove themselves not wrong, the officers offered to Jonathan Doody and Alex Garcia that they would try them as juveniles *if they would implicate the men from Tucson.* To be tried as a juvenile for a mass murder would have meant they would be out in about eight years, when they were 27 or 28 years old.

Garcia refused. He kept saying they had nothing to do with it, they weren't there. Jonathan Doody was willing to name them, but he hadn't paid enough attention to what was going on to be able to pick their faces out of a photo lineup, and it fell apart.

The drive to protect the incompetence, the poor training of the police when they make this kind of mistake, is overwhelming.

In the occasions I have seen, there's only one conclusion. *They would rather kill an innocent man than admit to having made a mistake,* because the politics of it simply mediate for that.

It isn't that they want to kill an innocent man to begin with, but once it gets going — once the police department becomes committed to it, the brass becomes committed to it, the prosecutor's office becomes committed to it — it gets easier because the responsibility spreads throughout the system. Everyone can say it's somebody else's fault, it's not my responsibility, let the jury decide.

This kind of moral corruption does not apply, by any means, to all police officers or to all prosecutors, or even to a substantial percentage of them, in my judgment.

Most of the prosecutors with whom I have worked recognize that they function as gatekeepers. Their job is to prosecute the guilty and protect the innocent.

Most police officers would be appalled at the idea of convicting an innocent.

Unfortunately, some officers, some prosecutors, when finding themselves embroiled in it, may not have the courage to reverse it — and some, as Mark Fuhrman would feel, don't give a damn — but this is the reality of it.

The need to tape record is there for a very simple reason. Under these kinds of pressures, badly trained as police are, they will produce coerced false confessions. There's no question about it, and the only protection for someone like Peter Reilly — or protection that would have been there for someone like Richard Lapointe — is the existence of the tape recording. Without that, their situations are virtually hopeless.

I have sat with people facing trial, facing murder charges that would result either in their spending the rest of their lives in jail or being executed, whose confessions were obtained. Some of these people were women whose infants, some newborn, had died of SIDS [Sudden Infant Death Syndrome] weeks after they were born. They were taken literally from the hospital where their children were pronounced dead, taken in for interrogation, made to confess.

In one case, the officer believed that the babies had died of exposure, so they got the woman to confess to intentionally putting the twins in an unheated room for the purpose of causing them to die of exposure. This was hours after they were pronounced dead.

When the autopsy showed that exposure could not possibly have been the cause and because the hospital staff was ignorant of the very rare phenomenon called simultaneous SIDS and, therefore, the police officers were ignorant of that, the same detectives went back to the same woman and now got her to confess to killing the babies in a different way. And had they needed a third, they could have gotten a third, and had they needed a fourth, they could have gotten a fourth; and she was convicted. They did not record the interrogation.

In Arkansas, there are three young men imprisoned, two of them for life plus forty or seventy years, one facing a death penalty.

Three 8-year-olds were killed in West Memphis, Arkansas. One had his penis cut off. The community was reasonably upset.

The police have no idea who did it. They fastened on a young man who, unfortunately, called himself Damien. They ended up bringing in someone who knew him from high school, a young man named Jesse Meskelly. Jesse was interrogated, unrecorded, and after a number of hours, after being told that there was evidence showing that he participated in the crime, after being given a polygraph and told that he flunked the polygraph, after being under enormous pressure, Jesse started to feed back to the police what they wanted to hear.

In the recorded part of the interrogation, they started to ask him about some aspects of the crime that had not been discussed, at which point Jesse revealed that he thought it happened at 9:00 o'clock in the morning. The three boys were in school and did not disappear until 5:30 in the afternoon.

Over the course of the interrogation, the police went back eight times and constantly moved the statement of when the crime happened from morning to the time about an hour after the kids disappeared.

In that case, the judge refused to allow testimony that false confessions even ever happened. He refused to let me testify about the

Bedau and Radelet *Stanford Law Review* article. He was not about to do anything that might allow the jury to think a false confession could happen, and there was no tape recording.

He refused to allow evidence to be presented about how false confessions come about and how it could have happened in this case. He refused to allow pointing out what indicated a false confession that was present in the testimony of the police, much less in the account of Jesse Meskelly. Meskelly was convicted and sentenced to spend the rest of his life in jail. Yet there's no way he could have committed this crime because he was thirty-five miles away in another town with half a dozen kids at an amateur wrestling arena. The jury heard their alibis for him, but they convicted him anyway. That is how powerful confession evidence is.

In my judgment, in the face of a trial — and we only get trials when the issue is in dispute, or when the defendant has more money than he knows what to do with, which rarely happens to the indigent defendants that I wind up appearing for — in a trial, the jury is under enormous pressure. My sense of what happens is that the jury is obviously conflicted with the authority of the state claiming the person did it. You have the state hammering away at usually ridiculous evidence suggesting that the person committed the crime, but making the centerpiece of it the confession. The jury also hears evidence suggesting that the person did not commit the crime, or the state failing to prove that they committed the crime. The jury is obviously conflicted.

Under those circumstances, it is possible to rationalize convicting a person by pointing to the confession and saying, "I wouldn't confess if I didn't do it," and that, the existence of the confession, I think, can resolve the conflict that can occur in the trial over the evidence.

The research on confession evidence shows that it is enormously important. It is very hard for jurors to disregard it. It contaminates a trial, so if we are going to let in confession evidence, we ought to make sure that it's good evidence.

Two states require that interrogations be recorded: Alaska and Minnesota.

In England, the law changed in 1984 so that all police interrogations must be recorded.

There are many police agencies around the United States that tape record for reasons of police professionalism. I review videotapes and audiotapes of interrogations that have been recorded in agencies that have adopted this rule, and the most amazing thing about them — not only do none of the techniques used against Richard Lapointe appear in these interrogations, none of the coercion, none of the threats, none of the impermissible police interrogation techniques — but the interrogators become skilled. They are much more effective. They do it properly and they do it well, *and they get statements that are reliable.* The minute an agency begins to record, the quality of police interrogation goes up. The quality of what's produced from an interrogation goes up, and the possibility of training interrogators to detect bad confessions early on now comes within the realm of possibility.

The two things I think that we need to do to reduce the number of convictions based on false confessions — false coerced confessions — are very simple: record the interrogation, and require police to produce corroboration for the confession.

Interrogations can be divided into two parts. It's very simple. The first part of a interrogation is designed to convince the person that he or she is caught, that the evidence is overwhelming, that there's no way that you will be able to convince me, the interrogator, that you didn't do this — and I essentially stand for the whole criminal justice system. If you can't convince me, you can't convince the prosecutor, you can't convince the judge, you can't convince the jury, and here is the evidence that proves it.

And if the person did commit the crime and the police have done their job right, there *is* substantial evidence; that's why they are interrogating him.

When the police are desperate, they do the same thing, except they fabricate all of the evidence. It's common for police to fabricate an element of evidence. If there is good reason to suspect someone, it will often happen that an eyewitness will be added in, because that sort of brings the person up over the hump so that they reach the conclusion that 'they got me.' Once the person has been moved to that point, eliciting the admission is easy. You don't have to use impermissible threats. Very minimal inducements are successful at eliciting the admission, once the person is convinced he is guilty.

If the police have no evidence and are simply, as Claude Rains would say [in *Casablanca*], "rounding up the usual suspects," *then they fabricate everything.* They fabricate fingerprints that don't exist, pubic hair found on the victim's body which is not there. They set up a polygraph and lie to the defendant and tell him that he flunked it and, therefore, his unconscious knows that he committed the crime.

In the face of that evidence, if you do not suspect that the police are capable of lying, you may do what Tom Sawyer did when he told the police in Clearwater, Florida, "I guess all the evidence is in; I guess I must have done this." It is the logical conclusion. That's what the interrogation is designed to produce, and it will work if the person is guilty. If the person is innocent, he may conclude that he is being railroaded, knowing he did not do it, and give what's called a *coerced-compliant false confession.* Or if, in addition to everything I mentioned, there is also an attack on the person's confidence in his memory, he may actually become persuaded that he committed a crime which he had nothing to do with.

When you tell Peter Reilly, "You were so upset about this that you repressed it," you are attacking his confidence in his memory that he did not commit the crime.

When you tell Tom Sawyer that the reason he doesn't remember killing Janet Staschek is that he used to be an alcoholic and it's possible to suffer dry blackouts — in the face of all this overwhelming evidence, he actually provisionally becomes convinced that he committed the crime.

When you tell George Abney, a graduate student at Northern Arizona University, that the reason he suffers depression, which he certainly knew he had a tendency to suffer, is because he is a multiple personality and one of his other personalities committed the crime, you have undercut his confidence in his memory — and it is only his memory that allows him to know that he did not do it, because the fabricated evidence says that he did.

And these are the two kinds of confessions that we usually see. In one case, coerced compliant, the person gives a confession knowing full well they are innocent, because they are exhausted and often because they have been put in the position of choosing whether to live or die.

In the other case, they have become persuaded temporarily that they committed the crime. At which point, they confess in the conditional and subjunctive tenses: I *must have*, I *would have* done this, *I did* that. They are confabulating the scenario of the crime.

In every case I have seen of a persuaded false confession, they confess in those tenses, using that grammar, because we all do it. When we accept something in principle that we have no memory of, we talk about it in the conditional and in the subjunctive, and that's what happens to people who are moved by these tactics of interrogation to do this. They would not do it alone, they do not go willingly, they are dragged, they are coerced, they are persuaded, they are terrorized into accommodating what the police want, and we permit it. We permit it because we do not require the police to tape record, and we do not require that they produce corroboration.

If someone, in fact, committed a crime and if, in fact, he is voluntarily giving a confession, there are thousands of questions that could be asked that would elicit actual knowledge of the crime. Not just what the police already know, but things the police don't know. And if you can elicit *that* from someone, you know they committed the crime. But we as a society do not require that, and police object to it. They object to it strenuously, and they object to it for only one reason: *because they wish to reserve to themselves the right to break the law when they choose to do it.*

There are more Mark Fuhrmans walking around out there wearing badges than any of us want to recognize. They are not all racists, but they are dangerous, and if we want to get rid of them and if we want to have the system work, *make them obey the law.* Make them accountable for what they do. And it's easily done: require a recording, and erect as a standard that you must produce corroboration.

Without corroboration, a confession must be considered highly suspect. There is no reason why, if someone committed a crime, corroboration cannot be elicited from them. It doesn't have to be an admission to something heinous. It can be the missing piece of clothing; describe in detail how it happened; come up with a narrative of the crime that is so detailed that it has internal surface validity. So it's obvious the person was there, it's obvious that they know about this, because what they say hangs together and is demonstrated by the facts.

That's not asking too much from the police, because if we don't demand that, perhaps as many as three out of five people in this room could be gotten to falsely confess if someone you know happens to die and the police have nobody better to suspect, and, of course, the more vulnerable the individual, the easier it is to do.

It's not that the logic of it changes. It's just that the ability to resist diminishes, and that's why we need to record interrogations.

Question Time

CHRIS POWELL, managing editor of the Journal Inquirer, *asks about the value of taping interrogations in light of the Peter Reilly case years ago and the current Johnny Lee Wilson case in Missouri. Both innocent suspects went to prison despite the existence of audiotapes that reveal psychological coercion. So where is the safeguard?*

OFSHE: The additional safeguard, I think, is substantial, because with the record, it's possible for a judge to suppress. Well, first of all, if it were tape-recorded, the likelihood of *producing* a coerced false confession would drop, in my judgment, to practically zero. Peter Reilly did not give that confession willingly. They had to threaten him.

The interrogations I review that come from Alaska, where this recording procedure has been in place for ten years, don't have these techniques as part of them. Police simply don't do it.

In the event that police *do* do it — as, for example, in Sacramento, where interrogations are routinely recorded — I recently testified in a case there in which it was perfectly obvious the interrogation should be suppressed, and the judge suppressed it.

In Flagstaff, Arizona, where another improper interrogation occurred, the transcript made it perfectly clear that it should be suppressed, and the judge — this was his first case after being appointed to the bench, he had been a prosecutor — he suppressed it, because it was the right thing to do.

If we give judges the evidence, I would like to believe that virtually all of them will do the right thing, so I think it makes a difference. And then it's also possible to explain to a jury how this happened and show a jury how, in the absence of any evidence connecting the person to the crime, we can explain why John Doe gave the statement he gave.

I think it makes a tremendous difference, and I think we would be much better off.

DIANE TWACHTMAN: I am a communication disorders specialist, so I'm well aware of the fact that there are many people who have language disabilities who are rather invisible. In other words, they might be able to answer in simple conversation, but when the language processing requirements become intense, they really break down under that pressure.

You have presented cases that, in my opinion, are very close to entrapment. When evidence is fabricated by police during interrogations, why isn't it considered entrapment the way it would be in other instances?

OFSHE: Because what gets fabricated in an interrogation is an overstatement of what the evidence is, and that's a technique that is simply tolerated, and I can understand why.

If there is a good basis to select someone for interrogation, from an interrogator's point of view, the ability to strengthen the case — if the theory I brought out about what leads people to confess is accurate, there's a logic to it, and the courts approve it. It's not up to me to pass judgment on whether or not it's a technique in the society we should allow. There's dispute about it, but it is, nevertheless, an allowed technique.

I don't think it is entrapment in the way we usually think about the term. It is a technique, it is a dangerous technique, and we can reduce the danger associated with it by recording.

TWACHTMAN: I think that's exactly what should be done. It seems so simple that one has to ask why isn't it being done. But I think in the case of a vulnerable person, in particular, the case could be made that, in fact, if you fabricate evidence and say that we have your polygraph results and your polygraph results tell us that you did this, et cetera, I think probably in the case of a vulnerable person, it really is very much entrapment.

OFSHE: I think it depends how you want to define the term *entrap-*

ment. It's deceptive, manipulative; it may be unfair; but whether the person appears to be vulnerable or not, being confronted with an authoritative, aggressive-in-demeanor police interrogator saying "I know you committed this crime" — this is a very upsetting experience for anyone.

Interrogation is a highly stressful experience, and one cannot appreciate it unless one has been there or listened to the full transcript or the full recording of an interrogation. It is not like anything that one has ever seen on television. It is a thousand times more intense. And so in England, for any suspect who is handicapped, either because of mental illness or because of intellectual handicap, it is required that an "appropriate adult" be present to make sure that precisely the thing you're talking about is not allowed to go too far.

The English are far more civilized about this thing than we are. It's amazing how it happened.

Prior to 1984 in England, police were not required to tape record. One case came up in which three adolescents were made to confess and were convicted of setting a fire that led to a death.

When the real arsonist was caught — I can't imagine this happening in the U.S. — but in England, because of this one case, because there was such public outrage and such press concern, because in this one case a false confession had been demonstrated, a royal commission was founded, research was done, new recommendations about police procedures were developed, were evaluated and were voted into place nationally in 1984 and they went into place in 1986, all because of one case.

In this country, it could never happen that way. There's a big difference.

Connecticut, hopefully, is a small enough state so that you can propose the legislation and make politicians stand up if they dare and say, "I'm in favor of convicting the innocent; I'm in favor of Mark Fuhrman; I'm in favor of lawless cops."

This is the age of Fuhrman. Now is the time to do it, because the reality of what some of us know goes on all the time is now available on CNN, and as we know, CNN controls the world.

The Ben Miller Frame-Up

John R. Williams

How I can retain any sense of optimism at all after the course of the last several decades in my own practice, I really don't know, and it's probably my own type of mental disability.

When Peter Reilly's original trial attorney came to me as the trial of that case was about to begin and, in despair, explained that the judge had denied the motion to suppress that confession — despite the tape recording, despite the obvious coercion and lack of reliability — I said, "Well, I don't think you have to worry. If you play that tape recording for a jury of ordinary Connecticut citizens, they will realize that that confession is unreliable and he will be acquitted."

The clouded crystal ball at work, I suppose.

I'm not going to talk about Richard Lapointe in the few minutes we have together today directly. I'm going to talk about Richard Lapointe by talking about another one of my mentally disabled clients who confessed to murders he did not commit, and his name is Ben Miller.

In Ben Miller's case, the evidence that proved he was innocent was also in the prosecutor's desk drawer the whole time. That prosecutor didn't die on the golf course, the way the state's attorney did who prosecuted Peter Reilly. He got promoted. He became the *chief* state's attorney and is now a judge in the Connecticut Superior Court. When his desk was cleaned out, they found proof of the person who actually had committed the murders of a series of prostitutes, all of

John Williams, famed as Connecticut's foremost civil rights attorney after a succession of high-profile cases exposing official misconduct, is representing Richard Lapointe pro bono *in his appeal to the Connecticut Supreme Court.*

whose bodies had been found in a parking area off the Merritt Parkway in the early seventies.

The proof existed because a state trooper driving along that road had caught another person in the act of committing an identical, carbon-copy crime to the ones for which Ben Miller was then in jail awaiting trial — and subsequent investigation by that trooper showed that that particular person had, indeed, been the last one seen with several of the women whom Ben Miller was alleged to have killed. That evidence was never disclosed.

John Williams.

Ben Miller was arrested because the cases were highly publicized. There was a great public outcry, a demand that they be solved. Allegations were made that the Stamford police and the Connecticut State Police were racists because they were not solving the crimes and the victims were all African-American, and for that reason, there was tremendous pressure to "solve the crime" — just as in the Lapointe case, just as in the Reilly case and in so many others.

They couldn't find anybody, and quite by accident in the course of interviewing people from the neighborhood, they stumbled across Ben Miller, who was a paranoid schizophrenic outpatient, working as a clerk in the post office in Darien, who in his off hours was a street-corner preacher in the neighborhood where many of these women practiced their trade.

It was obvious that he was not well, so it was arranged that a state employee, who was also a psychiatrist, would sign a commitment paper committing him to the Fairfield Hills State Hospital. Why? Because the superintendent of the Fairfield Hills State Hospital at that time, a man also named Miller, worked part-time for the State Police. He was considered the State Police surgeon, and he assured the State Police that if they would get this man committed to him, he would help them solve the crime. So they did get him committed, and he was medicated and Dr. Miller interrogated him for a period of days and then called the State Police and said, "Okay, he is ready for you."

The State Police came and obtained five written confessions to these murders. They arrested him and held a press conference announcing that they had solved all of these crimes. Dr. Miller then went to the public defender, who was about to be assigned to defend Mr. Miller, and said, "Now, I'm going to give you the victory of your life; if you retain me for this purpose, I will come to court and testify that your client was insane at the time he committed these terrible murders, and you'll win; he will be found not guilty by reason of insanity." And that is precisely what happened.

As a result, he was committed to Connecticut Valley State Hospital for the rest of his life as a criminally insane mass murderer.

But here's the rest of the story:

In 1979, I was in the Waterbury Superior Court defending Lorne Acquin. His confession to mass murder had been obtained by the same Lieutenant Shay — today the chief of police in East Hartford — who had obtained Peter Reilly's confession years earlier. But this time he was smart; he didn't use his tape recorder. He interrogated Acquin for eighteen hours before he confessed to those murders, the only evidence against him. Acquin was convicted, and his conviction was affirmed and he is in prison today.

During Acquin's trial, Ben Miller's mother came up to me in the hall of the court. She was in court herself because the State of Connecticut was suing her as her son's next of kin to make her pay for his incarceration at Connecticut Valley State Hospital, and she thought that was a bit much.

So I agreed to help her, and as a result she didn't have to pay the bill. But in the course of that, she asked me if I would look into her son's case. I agreed to do it, and in an attic in a State Police building in Meriden after about a year of work, I located several, literally, dust-covered boxes that contained, among other things, all the material from the state's attorney's desk drawer that proved conclusively the identity of the real killer, and that Ben Miller's confessions, all five of them — which, by the way, didn't fit the known evidence — were false.

So I filed an action in the Superior Court of Middletown, a habeas corpus action to obtain his release, and we proved all of these things. All of the witnesses testified, all of the stories I have told you were proven, and the judge found that they were proven — and he ruled against us, because, he said, *our client had been found not guilty* by reason of insanity. In other words, "You won, justice has been done, case dismissed."

I appealed to the appellate court. The appellate court, in an opinion written by then-Judge, later Justice, T. Clark Hull — a known civil libertarian, a respected man — said, "Dismissal affirmed; he was found not guilty by reason of insanity; he is at Whiting Forensic Institute; he's a prisoner in a psychiatric hospital; he has been vindicated."

I appealed to the Connecticut Supreme Court. They refused even to hear the case. I filed a habeas corpus in the federal court, Chief Judge Ellen Burns. A fine human being, brilliant judge. Same ruling: you lose, go away, we don't want to reopen the case.

I went down to New York, and as luck would have it, purely by chance, was heard by a panel of three judges. The presiding judge was Amelia Kurs, who was appalled. She wrote a decision requiring that the conviction be set aside, the rulings be set aside, and that Miller be given a new trial. The State of Connecticut immediately dismissed all charges. Ben Miller, having been a prisoner for almost two decades, was released.

But he will never be compensated for the time he lost. The tardive dyskinesia from which he suffers is the result of the Thorazine with which he was so heavily medicated during the time that he was at Whiting. It has left lifelong effects, and he will never be the same.

Those who did him wrong continue to hold high office in the state of Connecticut.

These cases are many. They are not old cases. They are not in other states. They are here and now, and there will be another one tomorrow. I do not believe anything other than firm rules will ever change that circumstance. In the Lapointe case, among other things, we are asking Connecticut to adopt and enforce the rule of Alaska and Minnesota that there be a recording made of all police interrogations. And I hope we win that, and it will help, but it will not solve the problem.

I think that Arthur Miller is close when he suggests an application of the English practice. I firmly believe that nothing less than an absolute prophylactic rule that provides that confessions *will not be received in evidence* unless the person confessing had the assistance of counsel at the time he or she confessed — nothing less than that will solve the problem we are addressing today. Will we ever get such a rule? Well, that would show that we were *soft on crime*, wouldn't it? And we can't be soft on crime.

There's a profound ignorance and a profound hypocrisy abroad in the land, and I don't know the answer to that problem, but I hope some of you will be able to help us find that solution here today and in the days ahead. Thank you for all that you're doing.

The Reasons for "Wrong-Man" Cases

Kate Germond

I feel I should tell you a little bit about our organization. It's called Centurion Ministries because the man who started the work was a businessman who had a spiritual awakening. He didn't really know what to do with it because he never had one before, so he enrolled in Princeton Theological Seminary, and there, as a product of his seminary work, he did prison outreach work for his field education program, and there he met a man who told him a provocative story of his innocence.

What you should understand about this man, Jim McCloskey, my boss, is that he was right-wing; he was the opposite of a liberal. In fact, when Martin Luther King died, he said, "Good, now we are rid of that troublemaker" — so this is not a man who entered this work wide-eyed and liberal, as probably I did.

This Hispanic man told him a provocative story of his innocence. Jim came to believe he was innocent, so he dropped out of seminary, used his own money to investigate the case, got the chief witness against him to come forward and tell the truth, hired a lawyer, filed a habeas petition, and the man was freed and vindicated from a life sentence for a murder he didn't commit. That was the beginning of Centurion Ministries in 1980.

Since that time, we have freed and vindicated sixteen people who were serving life or death sentences for crimes they did not commit. We are a tiny little organization. There are only three of us. Jim and I do the investigations, and we have an office administrator.

One of the things I wanted to touch on — I realize this conference is primarily about coerced confessions, but in our experience, we have come across a number of other themes that lead to wrongful convictions. Professor Bedau and Constance Putnam spoke a little bit about them, and I wanted to probably revisit them for those of you who could use a further education in wrongful convictions.

One of the things that we see predominantly is the use of jailhouse informants, with a subsequent plea agreement for this false testimony.

One of the things that Professor Ofshe mentioned as a stopgap to coerced confessions is corroborating evidence. My response to that would be that *what the prosecutors and the police usually provide as corroborating evidence is jailhouse informants.*

You have the person who confesses falsely, and you put him in a jail cell. And then you have sleazy people who need to make deals to get the most precious commodity when you are incarcerated, which is freedom — you get them to say that this person confessed to them as well, so there's your corroborating evidence. It's not physically at the crime scene, but it's the word of another person. And to a lot of us who are not sitting in a courtroom, it seems inconceivable that anybody would believe some person with a long criminal record, who is going to walk away from these crimes for this testimony — but they do. It has a profound effect on juries.

Eyewitness identification. In practically every single one of our cases, there's been a wrong identification by an eyewitness. I read somewhere that Elizabeth Loftus, who is one of the preeminent authorities on eyewitness identification, said that the miracle is when you get it right, not that you get it wrong.

In a crime situation, the stakes are high; there's a lot going on. The chances of somebody remembering what a person looked like who is perpetrating a crime against them is going to be remote. Or an eyewitness who sees a person just run by — they are not going to remember what that person looks like. But people come up with descriptions — which are convenient, usually, to fit the person who has been arrested. And that usually involves police encouragement, if not outright coercion.

Racism. Racism is a big theme. Almost all the people who apply

KATE GERMOND — associate of James McCloskey, the founder of Centurion Ministies in Princeton, New Jersey — is a nationally known investigator of miscarriages of justice.

to us are people of color; and then the folks who aren't are poor, and I think that's a form of racism. We seem to have the same disdain for the poor as we do for people of color in our courts.

All of our cases have been pressure-cooker cases. The police were under pressure from the community to solve the crime quickly, so there's a rush to judgment. All of our defendants or all of our clients, there was pretty much a reason why they were arrested or questioned in the first place, but shortly after intense questioning, and as information developed about the actual crime, it had to have become obvious to the police that they had the wrong person. And at that point, a conscious decision is made to go forward with the wrongful conviction.

It's there that I beg to differ with Dr. Bedau and Constance Putnam. *I don't believe it's a mistake that these wrongful convictions occur.* I believe that at some point, the police and the prosecutor conspire to frame an innocent person, and that's what's dead wrong about this. It would be one thing if they were innocent errors and the system just sort of screwed up a little bit and this person accidentally went to jail, but that isn't what happens. It's a conscious effort, and that's dead wrong.

And then the final insult in this whole process is that frequently the clients, because they are indigent, are given inexperienced lawyers. And even if the lawyers are experienced, they don't have the financial backing to put on an O.J. Simpson defense, so justice is once again compressed and the system just grinds up this person. Careers are made on the backs of innocent people who are wrongfully convicted.

I think I don't need to go on and on. You have heard a lot of stories about wrongful convictions. If during the Q&A you have questions, we can discuss cases.

One of the things people ask is, what can we do to change this? At Centurion Ministries we believe it necessary is to abolish the use of plea bargains. If somebody is dying to tell the truth about what he knows about a crime or a person who has committed a crime, why should he be rewarded for doing this? We should just abolish plea bargains. I think that would put quite a few holes in cases.

In England, they don't allow eyewitness testimony if it can't be corroborated by other evidence, and we have a lot of cases where the conviction rests strictly on eyewitness identification, and the eyewitnesses were dead wrong. People have served a lot of years in prison because a person made an honest mistake. But I must also add that these *honest mistakes* are usually encouraged by the police who have this blind focus and want the victim or an eyewitness to identify the specific person.

Finally, I think there should be accountability. As it is now in most states, once you have been freed and vindicated, you cannot sue the police officer who framed you or the prosecutor who buried the evidence. In most cases, these folks just continue to move up the ladder. The police officer becomes a detective, and then becomes a detective in the prosecutor's office; the prosecutor becomes a senator, and on and on it goes. I think there should be some accountability, and that can only happen from the community.

Why Johnny Lee Wilson Went to Prison

Michael Atchison & Denis W. Keyes

[ATCHISON:]

Don Connery mentioned earlier in the day that he hoped through this conference and other activity that Richard Lapointe will become the most famous innocent man in prison in America. I suspect right now, at this moment, that Johnny Wilson may have that distinction, if you can call it a distinction. Hopefully, very soon, he will be the most famous innocent person who *used* to be in prison.

Unlike everybody else who has spoken to you before today, we are going to sit here and chat, and Denis is going to chime in with some of the psychological stuff that he does. I'm going to lay out the facts for you.

Johnny Wilson is a 30-year-old man with mental retardation who is serving a life sentence for a murder he did not commit. Johnny grew up in the small southwest Missouri town of Aurora, a town of six thousand people, and for those of you who don't have any idea of Missouri/Kansas/Oklahoma geography, it is literally in the middle of nowhere. It's on the edge of the Ozarks.

In 1986, Johnny was twenty years old and living at home with his mother and grandmother. Johnny has barely known his father his entire life.

On April 13th, 1986, a 79-year-old woman named Pauline Martz, well-known and loved in the community, was killed. Someone broke into her house, bound her up with duct tape and burned her house down around her.

Johnny and his mother that afternoon had been at the local grocery store, had heard the sirens and the fire trucks go by, and like many of the folks in Aurora, went to the fire to see what had happened. They hung around there well into the evening like hundreds of other residents did, nobody then really knowing what had happened inside.

Johnny has mental retardation, never had a driver's license, quiet guy, kept to himself, never a discipline problem, did odd jobs in the community, mowed some lawns for friends of his grandmother's and his mother's.

On the following Friday, the 18th of April, Johnny was picked up by the police based on a single tip from another person with mental retardation in Aurora, a man named Gary Wall, who said to police that Johnny at the fire scene had indicated to him that Johnny's brother had been involved.

Johnny is an only child, which should give you some indication where this is going.

Friday night, the police picked Johnny up at the local movie theater, ostensibly to identify a lost wallet. They took him back to the police station, and at 8:30 they began a four-hour interrogation. Johnny was read his Miranda rights, waived his right to counsel, and they were off to the races.

About two hours later, after he had denied being involved in this murder more than thirty times, the pressure heated up. The police became more and more confrontational. They indicated to Johnny that they knew he did it, that they had witnesses, that there was laboratory analysis, there were all of these things. Johnny at that point became very scared and very confused, and he made up a story and said that he and two other young men from Aurora had been involved, that he had initially gone along for the ride and watched this happen, and the story developed more and more the harder they pushed him.

About an hour later, the police out of nowhere told Johnny, "We know they weren't involved; we know that you did it by yourself; it's

MICHAEL ATCHISON, working pro bono with David Everson, a fellow attorney with Stinson, Mag & Fizzell of Kansas City, Missouri, has sought the freedom of Johnny Lee Wilson, a youth who falsely confessed to murder. DENIS W. KEYES, a psychologist and special education professor at the University of Charleston in South Carolina, took part in the Wilson case as a specialist in the vulnerabilities of mentally disabled suspects.

time to come clean," and so he said, "Okay, I did it."

I have a couple of excerpts from the interrogation. Unlike the Lapointe case, we have the whole thing on tape, but that doesn't necessarily keep you out of prison for nine and a half years. I'm about to show you my stone-age audiovisual.

I don't know how well you can see these words so I'm going to read them for you. This is an excerpt from the four-hour interrogation.

The officer says to Johnny, "Okay, whenever you looked in and you seen Mrs. Martz tied, gagged, laying on the floor, what was she wearing? What did you see?"

Johnny says, "A blouse of some sort. I can't tell what color."

The officer: "Try to think. These little details are important, and it's important that you tell the true story as most accurate as possible because that will show that you're trying to tell the truth. This is an important time."

Johnny says, "I'll say it was white, probably a white or bluish blouse."

The officer: "Okay. How about bluish? I'll go for that."

Johnny: "Yeah."

Officer: "How about bluish green maybe?"

Johnny: "Yeah."

That's not really the best one, though. As I indicated before, Mrs. Martz had been bound with duct tape, and Johnny knew that she had been tied up. That became pretty well known pretty soon. Officers had told him that, but when they tried to find out what she was bound up with, Johnny's inability to offer real details shows.

The officer says, "What besides a rope was around her ankles? Something else. This is another test. I know and you know. Just think. Come on, John."

Johnny: "I'm thinking."

"What are some things that could be used?"

"Handcuffs, I think."

"No, no. Wrong guess. What are some things you could tie somebody up with? A rope is all that he had, but that tells me something, John. That tells me something. That tells me something. I told you it's important that you are straight with me. You took the tape up there."

"Huh?"

"You took the tape up there, didn't you?"

"I didn't have anything with me. I didn't have tape or anything. I think Chris had the tape."

The Chris he mentions is one of the other two young men that he said were involved with him.

Johnny throughout his interrogation was unable to provide any details of the crime that weren't first provided to him by the police. There are instances like this all throughout the interrogation, leading questions, yes, no, that sort of thing. And with that, I will let Denis talk a little bit about what it is about Johnny that really put him in serious jeopardy the day of the interrogation.

[KEYES:]

Regrettably, another important point of that is that there was evidence at the crime scene that was exposed to Johnny. There was a stun gun that was found among the burned objects in the room very near to where Mrs. Martz was lying, and the police brought the stun gun in to show Johnny. And they had it behind him, I believe, they were standing behind him, and they shot the stun gun — not at him, but they shot the stun gun — and said, "What's that, Johnny?" and he goes, "A razor thing, I think."

An electric razor. He thought it was an electric razor. He had no idea what it was, and the evidence, throughout the entire case, the evidence just did not hold up.

What helped to convict Johnny Wilson was that he is mentally retarded. People with mental disabilities effectively come to the criminal justice system unarmed and ill-equipped. They possess characteristics in their intellectual abilities, social abilities, that are often deadly when they are dealing with the police, and you have to understand that people who are mentally disabled oftentimes — all of the time, really, are taught that the police are our friends, that they are the people we should trust to help us when we need help, and when you've got a problem, who do you call?

They don't understand the dangers that may exist in any interrogation situation from police who have always been their friends. They are completely vulnerable in this situation, and the question of their competence cannot be avoided. We have to question their competence.

Johnny did not understand the Miranda rights. In addition to his intellectual disability and social disability, he has a verbal comprehension, verbal language disability, so that he not only doesn't understand what he is hearing, but he is often unable to answer correctly for what he does hear, for what he processes.

He didn't understand his Miranda rights. 'You have the right to waive these rights, do you waive them?' Well, to Johnny, *waiving his rights* might have been waving to the right or a wave on the sea.

He didn't understand the cause-and-effect situation he was in, that if he said something, it could come back to haunt him. He didn't know that. All he knew is that he was terrified, he was absolutely terrified, and he didn't know why they were doing this to him — and these were people that he knew, too. He had seen these people around the community. This is a small town.

He was also — he *is* extremely concrete. He believes in very concrete thought. He is only able to think in concrete thought. Abstractions to him are just not something he could understand.

He is extremely suggestible. There's research going on right now that is going to be introduced later on by Dr. Greenspan that is very important research regarding the suggestibility of people with mental disabilities, and I think that this is something that he will talk about a lot more.

One of the reasons that I asked to get involved in this case was to explain how Johnny could have come up with a confession.

Now, Johnny didn't have to come up with a confession. He didn't have to at all, because it was fed to him word by word. He didn't have to say, "I did this," because they said, "You did it, didn't you?"

Now, people with mental retardation are likely to acquiesce in these situations. They want to please the person who is asking the questions. They want to be accepted as "normal" in those situations. Therefore, they will be inclined to give the person the answer he wants, so a lot of the importance here is on how these questions are formed. If they are formed as, "You did this, didn't you?," the person is likely to go, "Yes, because you want me to say yes."

The suggestibility factor is extremely important in all confessions by people with mental disabilities, because they want to be accepted; they want to be regarded as normal.

In Johnny's case, there was a whole lot of information in the confession, but there wasn't a whole lot to go on for how he came up with the stuff that he did come up with.

My working with him was to take a test called the Thematic Apperception Test, also known as a TAT. It's a technique wherein you use cards with free-form designs to get the person to give you information. You show them a card and ask them to tell a story about the card. The story should have a beginning, a middle and an end. The middle should represent the picture, and the person should tell what happened before that and after. With the first couple of cards, I didn't say anything to Johnny. I held them up, and all he was able to do was give a cursory description.

After that, I started asking him some real simple questions about people in the card and what happened before that and who is this person and that kind of thing, and it didn't take very long and Johnny started talking, and he made up little stories to go with my questions. This, to me, was enough evidence that I could say he is suggestible. So much so in this situation that he was able to come up with stories that made sense instead of just the cursory descriptions, because he was willing to help me get the information that I wanted, and that's, I believe, what happened in his interrogation.

[ATCHISON:]
Okay. So far, we have a confession, and Johnny is not convicted of anything yet. Johnny never went to trial. Johnny pleaded guilty to this crime. Johnny was very afraid of receiving the death penalty.

At the time of the confession, the only evidence in this case that anybody really knew about was this confession, and Johnny, his lawyers, the prosecutor, all believed that if — well, maybe they all believed he was guilty except Johnny, but they *all* believed if he went to trial, based on his confession, he would be convicted and he would receive the death penalty — so he entered a guilty plea, and let me read a little bit of the plea colloquy.

The court asked Johnny, "Why are you pleading guilty, Johnny?"
"I don't know."
"Pardon?"
"I don't know."
"You don't know why you're pleading guilty?"
"Just for first-degree murder."

"Well, that's what you're pleading guilty to, but why are you wanting to enter that plea?"

"I don't know."

"Do you want to enter a plea of guilty?"

"Yes."

"Why do you want to enter a plea of guilty?"

(No response.)

"You can go ahead and talk to me."

"I don't know."

"Do you know that the death penalty is a possibility in this case?"

"Yes."

"Do you want the death penalty?"

"No."

"Do you want to avoid the death penalty?"

"Yes."

"Are you admitting that you committed this murder?"

"Yes."

I think at his plea hearing, the death penalty was mentioned about eighteen times. At one point, the judge told him, "You know, if you don't plead guilty, you can go to trial and there is a slim chance you won't get the death penalty," so Johnny went to prison.

We have picked apart the confession and told you why the confession doesn't support his guilt. There are other things about it. They told Johnny he must have taken some things from this house, so he said he took some jewelry and he told them exactly where he put it. He said he put it in a barbecue pit at his house. The police went there and it wasn't there.

[KEYES:]
They ripped the barbecue down brick by brick and it wasn't there.

[ATCHISON:]
They searched his house and took some of his mother's underwear and said it had to be Pauline Martz' underwear, that sort of thing. But perhaps the most spectacular and unusual part about this case is that after Johnny went to prison, *somebody else* confessed.

He was a man named Chris Brownfield. The police initially heard of him two days after the killing, when an officer from another local town called and said, "This sounds like a crime that Chris Brownfield could have committed, you ought to check into him."

Brownfield wrote a letter from prison and said, "I did this crime in Aurora, Missouri." They wrote back and said, "We've got somebody in jail, we don't believe you." He wrote them back and said, "Well, I bet you found a stun gun at the fire." That got their attention, because that was never publicly disclosed.

Brownfield, for whatever reason, has maintained that he did this thing, and he has been fairly cooperative. He has maintained through the last seven years that he committed this crime, and there are telephone records and motel records and witnesses that all corroborate this.

There was a young woman named Melanie Houser who, at the time, was 13 years old. Mrs. Martz' house was adjacent to the local high school football field and track. Melanie saw a person go to Mrs. Martz' door about the time of the murder. She later identified Chris Brownfield in a photo lineup and identified his car. Another woman in the community, Lucille Childress, later said she saw Johnny and his mother at the grocery store at the time the sirens raced past, going to the fire.

Gary Wall, who had initially implicated Johnny, has recanted his statement, saying the police used the same sort of tactics on him that they did on Johnny. It is a remarkably compelling case, and you couldn't write it any better — but nine and a half years later, Johnny is still in prison, which indicates one of two things: either I am a very bad lawyer, which may be the case, but I know the guy I am with is a very good lawyer, so these things are just incredibly hard to persuade people about.

The one thing that people bring up over and over again when they hear about this case, and you have heard this time and time again today, is: *Why would a person who didn't commit a murder say he did?* People have no concept of it at all, but the more you explain to people, the more you show them cases like this case and the Melvin Reynolds case that was talked about before, and the Tom Sawyer case, you see the recurring theme and it does get people's attention.

Johnny Wilson's case has been to the Missouri Supreme Court once. That was before my firm actually had the case. We lost there. We have asked the governor of the state of Missouri to give Johnny a pardon, and this has been going on for better than a year now. I will give them this: they have done what appears to be a remarkably thorough investigation. They are, I really believe, trying to get to the bottom of things and do the right thing.

Just one other thing I would like to say. There's been a lot talk today about police and prosecutors and the like. I think the vast majority of the folks in law enforcement are good public servants trying to do the best they can. In virtually every one of these cases, though, it breaks down, and it's not just on the police. Lawyers make mistakes, defense lawyers make mistakes, judges make mistakes, police officers make mistakes. In this case, *everybody* made mistakes, and that's why Johnny Wilson is in prison now.

We have been the beneficiaries of really terrific help from the media. Joe Shapiro at *U.S. News and World Report* wrote a wonderful article that Bob Perske hounded him into doing. That started the ball rolling. *20/20* did a piece that aired last March. Connie Chung has done a couple of broadcasts.

We have gotten a lot of help from a lot of regular folks, from within the state of Missouri and from all over the country. They get fired up about this and respond to these very basic issues of justice. They get very passionate about them and write the governor lots and lots of letters. And if you want to help Richard Lapointe and you don't know how to do it, just start putting pressure on the public officials, because I know that helped in the Wilson case.

[KEYES:]
One last thing. Regarding mental retardation and the criminal justice system, I am firmly convinced that the law enforcement agencies, the prosecutors, the defense attorneys, et cetera, have to be informed about what to look for when they are interrogating someone and before they are interrogating someone. They have to be able to look and see that this person may have a mental disability that would essentially make it impossible for them to be reliable in an interrogation. If all that had happened, Richard Lapointe and Johnny Wilson would not be in the situation they are in now.

The 22-Year Ordeal of Mike Pardue

E. Barry Johnson & Becky Pardue

[BARRY JOHNSON:]

In 1973, 22 years ago, the same year that Peter Reilly was arrested, local police in a small town — Saraland, Alabama — solved three murders by blaming and forcing a 17-year-old boy to confess. Michael Pardue is that boy's name. He is now 39, and he is still in prison.

At the time, Mike had a 9th grade education, a learning disability and no parents. The year before his arrest, his father, a severe alcoholic who had abused Mike his whole life, physically and verbally, came home one night drunk to their house trailer — they were very poor — and shot and killed his mother. She died in Mike's arms when he was sixteen years old.

Between that and the learning disability he suffered from and his child abuse, he was particularly susceptible to the interrogation that he would face. It was an 80-hour interrogation stretching over four days. *Eighty hours!*

Two of the three murders occurred on May 21st, 1973. At the time, Mike was living with his grandmother and younger brother and sister. He had dropped out of school and was cutting yards, helping to feed the family.

E. BARRY JOHNSON, attorney amd trial counsel with the Federal Defender Program in Montgomery, Alabama, is currently working pro bono *on behalf of Michael Pardue, imprisoned as a teenager in 1973 after falsely confessing to three murders. BECKY PARDUE, a Mobile, Alabama businesswoman, met Pardue in 1983, soon changed her name to his after learning of his wrongful imprisonment, and finally was able to marry him in 1988. She has spent a dozen years fighting through the courts for his freedom.*

The police called him on May 22nd and asked him to come to the police station. They had found his car with a flat tire and two stolen tires in the back seat — tires which he had, in fact, taken. He voluntarily went to the police station on May 22nd, and he never came home. They never called his grandmother to tell her they were interrogating him. Two attorneys came to the jail to see him specifically and were turned away on two different occasions.

He was interrogated throughout the days of the 22nd, 23rd, 24th and 25th. He was beaten. He was deprived of food and sleep. After 80 hours of interrogation, we have a tape-recorded statement and confession to killing two gas station attendants who had been murdered on the night of May 21st — really the early morning hours of May 22nd. The victims were named Harvey Hodges and Ronald Rider.

Whoever did kill these people, it obviously was the same person. The same type of birdshot from a gun, a double-barreled shotgun. The murders were closely related in distance, although in different counties — which has caused us an enormous problem because the cases are on different tracks because of the different counties — and both gas stations were robbed.

While Mike was being interrogated, they found a decomposed body on the side of the road. The forensic report — I have it right here — states that they can't determine the cause of death, but the victim had been dead about five weeks. Mike confessed to that, too, so we have three murders.

The primary interrogator in this case was a man named Bill Travis. He was the chief detective in the Mobile County sheriff's department. They had Baldwin County, Mobile County and Saraland police tag teams interrogating a 17-year-old boy.

Two attorneys who tried to see Mike at that time have testified under oath that when they went there, the atmosphere was hostile. They instructed the police to cease interrogating him immediately, and they were turned away. Bill Travis, now dead, was well known for solving his cases with a dead body and a confession. We have had a little bit of difficulty getting people who worked with him to admit that, but they will admit it off the record. We have had other people that will admit it. He was subsequently fired for beating supposedly over a hundred and fifty people, and he admitted under oath in 1973 that he had a reputation for beating young suspects. That's in the trial transcript.

On the fifth day of the interrogation, a young boy by the name of Johnny Brown came into the Saraland jail to pay a traffic fine. Mike had been with Johnny Brown on the night of the murders but had not implicated him at this point. Travis saw Brown and grabbed him and took him in a room. He was with his stepfather at the time, but he didn't let the stepfather in the room. Travis told Brown if he would just admit that he had seen Mike that night with a gun and some money, and that his clothes had been bloody, he would let him go home.

Brown continued to state that he had not seen Mike with a gun that night, he had not seen him with any money, and he had not seen him with any blood on his clothes.

Brown's family came down to the jail to check on him when he didn't come home, and they hired a lawyer that night. The lawyer finally made Travis bring Brown out in the hall. He brought him out in the hall with his arm around him and said, "He will be home in twenty minutes. He is not a suspect."

In fact, he remained there, and eventually *he* spent thirteen years in prison as well. That night, he remained in the jail the entire night while they interrogated him, in a separate room from Michael, until 4:30 in the morning. Brown was subsequently transferred to another jail. Three days later, he was beaten so severely that his lawyer came to the jail, took pictures, and called a doctor to examine him. At Brown's trial in October of 1974, his lawyer testified about his injuries. The photographs of his injuries were introduced to the judge, to the court in the suppression hearing.

Brown's cellmate testified that he had to help him on to the bed and that he could hear him screaming all the way down the hall. And the doctor who examined him testified. Nonetheless, the judge let the confession in, and as a result Brown was convicted and sent to prison.

John Brown was paroled thirteen years later, and now he's dying. He lives in Irvington, Alabama. He still cannot read or write, and he couldn't then. He's got a fourth-grade education. He has every reason to resent Mike Pardue, because Mike was forced to implicate him after 80 hours of interrogation. He's dying and has no reason to lie. He maintains his innocence to this day and Mike's innocence as well.

Michael Pardue had two trials. Or he was *scheduled* to have two trials. The first trial was in August of '73, several months after the arrest, in Baldwin County.

He had an attorney who had been out of law school two years and basically did nothing for him. One federal judge has already determined that this attorney rendered ineffective counsel in the Baldwin County case. The trial lasted an hour and a half. The trial transcript is just sixty pages long. The defense attorney called one witness, his aunt, who testified that he had been acting a little strange ever since his mother died.

They introduced a gun — this is the most amazing part — at the trial as the murder weapon. All during that four-day interrogation, Mike could not lead them to one scrap of physical evidence to connect him to the crime. He kept sending them on false leads about a gun at his grandmother's house, in a creek behind the police station, everywhere, but they couldn't find anything. They seized his clothes; no blood. By the way, both murder scenes were extremely gory, and the cases were very high-profile, on the front page of the paper every day. I have the articles. Anybody who was there would have been covered in blood. They seized his clothes; no blood. They searched his car; no blood. No physical evidence from either crime scene was found on Mike or his clothes.

At the trial, they introduced the murder weapon. At some point during the interrogation, Mike finally said he used a sawed-off shotgun that he had retrieved from his aunt and uncle's house. They are now dead. Their names were J.B. and Effie Mae Duncan. Elizabeth, their daughter, who was 14 at the time and is an extremely credible person, does not want to get involved. She's shy and very nervous about this whole thing, but she vividly recalls the police coming to her house to seize this gun.

It was in a closet that was off of her bedroom. If Mike had used this gun, he would have had to sneak in their house — which was about eighteen hundred square feet — in the middle of the night, steal a gun, go on a killing spree, return to the house without waking anyone up, and be at his grandmother's that morning.

When the police seized the gun, it had cobwebs and spiders on it. They said, "This cannot be the gun; it hasn't been fired in months," but they confiscated it anyway because it was sawed off and illegal. The Duncans were never told that that was the gun used to convict

Mike. Nelson Grubbs, the toxicologist, testified at the trial that when Sheriff Travis brought him the gun for examination, it was cleaned and freshly oiled; it had no fingerprints on it.

The Duncans found out only as recently as 1988 that *that* was the supposed murder weapon. They never knew it.

Michael was convicted of that murder in Baldwin County. Three months later, in the Mobile case, which was about the other dead gas station attendant as well as a decomposed body that had been found elsewhere, Mike Pardue was told that if he didn't plead guilty in light of his other conviction, he would get the death penalty. In fact, he was told, "We will see your ass fried in the electric chair."

The death penalty was unconstitutional in 1973. His lawyer didn't tell him otherwise because *he didn't know*, and we have that in an affidavit. He now realizes that the death penalty was unconstitutional and has recanted that statement, but we have it in an affidavit that he completed at the request of a federal judge who was trying to figure out why he did all these things.

Oh, by the way. The same attorney withdrew the appeal of the Baldwin County case three months after he filed it, without telling Mike.

On the day that Mike was scheduled to go to trial on October 24, 1973, he pled guilty to the decomposed body and to the death of the gas station attendant and three counts of grand larceny. He was not told he had a right to appeal those convictions as well; he found that out later and filed appeals.

After he exhausted his appeals over the years, he filed habeas petitions in 1990 and won in both cases, which is amazing. And last May, he was re-tried on the Hodges murder and the death of Theodore Roosevelt White, the decomposed body murder, and won.

The White killing is not even on his tape-recorded confession back in 1973. That was just an oral confession he supposedly gave at some point after 80 hours. They do have the tape-recorded confession of the Hodges and the Rider murders. There are two things about it that are particularly enlightening.

One is that during the confession, Mike has one lucid moment where he is really telling the truth. He had stolen a truck that night, and he saw police cars fly by, and Travis asked on the tape-recorded confession, "Mike, what did you think when you saw those police go by?"

He said, "I done thought I got busted for stealing a sorry-ass car." The police replied, "You didn't think about that man you just killed?" And he said, "No, I didn't think I could've hardly done anything like that."

Another time, he's asked whether the victim in Baldwin County, Rider, had a hat on when he shot him. He said, "I can't recall, but I seen a picture of him with a hat on." He was being shown pictures throughout the interrogation.

Anyway, we had a trial last May. We had won *pro se habeas* relief, and the state had 180 days to retry him. So they retried him in May on the Hodges murder, the Mobile County murder. The judge, who was the district attorney until about two years ago, let in the tape-recorded confession again. The jury convicted him solely on the basis of that confession.

We're now on appeal in that case, and I have absolutely no doubt it will be overturned. The Baldwin County murder was scheduled to be tried in August. Again, the only evidence they have is the confession, and so it has been indefinitely stayed, pending the appeal of the Mobile County case to see if the confession will be ruled inadmissible. And that's where we are.

[BECKY PARDUE:]
I met Mike Pardue ten years into his incarceration, in 1983. Despite the brutality of his imprisonment — and believe me, in 1973, Alabama's maximum security prisons were brutal. He was a teenager, very small framed, and he had a very, very hard time in prison — despite this, despite his horrific childhood, I found Michael Pardue to be an extremely gentle person, very sensitive, a kind human being and simply the finest person I have ever met.

Our relationship grew, despite the barriers of our separation and his being in prison. We made a commitment to each other and a commitment to his freedom.

At that point, we were naive enough to believe that parole was a possibility for him. After all, he had an excellent institutional record, he had gained minimum custody, we had taken fourteen eight-hour passes away from prison without incident. He had an excellent job on the state cattle ranch. He was a prison cowboy and a good one.

We were so sure that parole was coming that I went out and

bought going-home clothes for Michael.

Within months of our parole hearing, the Department of Corrections passed a new rule governing consecutive life sentences, prisoners with consecutive life sentences, which Michael had at the time. They said that no prisoner with consecutive life sentences would be able to have minimum custody.

The result of this was that, overnight, Mike lost his job on the cattle crew; he lost his minimum custody; and we lost our passes and everything that we had worked for. Our hope just went down the drain in one fell swoop.

Because he was so good at his job, the state foreman of the cattle ranch talked the warden into allowing Mike to continue to come out and work the cattle on the ranch, because they needed him. So Mike would get up every morning and work the cattle, get on the horse, ride the state property and continue to work.

One day while he was out, another inmate came up to Michael — a man who was, in fact, guilty of murder and rape — and said, "Hey, Pardue, I just got my parole papers; how about that?"

Well, Mike, being innocent of the crimes, being desperately depressed over what had happened with our passes and our custody, simply found this unbearable.

He rode his horse to the assistant warden's home. There was no one there. He knew it, because he knew how the warden came and went. He broke in and he took the warden's keys. He took a gun, and he took a walkie-talkie so he could hear what was going on in the police jurisdiction, and he took the car. He escaped in the warden's Corvette. Needless to say, the warden was not pleased about that.

It was quite a sensational thing in Alabama: a mad triple murderer escaping from prison, armed and dangerous, running amuck. Lock your windows, put your children away in the house.

What, in fact, happened was that the Corvette didn't have any gas. He took the gun up the hill to a service station about fifteen miles away from the prison and traded it — after first removing the bullets. This mad murderer didn't hold up the service station; he traded the empty gun for gas for the Corvette.

He went and spent a day and a half with his dying father, and subsequently was arrested. He was not very good at escaping; he had run away two times before a decade earlier and was soon caught.

Once again he was brought back to prison without incident.

As a result of this latest non-violent escape, Michael was tried and given a life sentence without the possibility of parole.

At that point, we knew we only had two options. We could either give up and die, or we could fight. We chose to fight. We knew at that point that there was not much of a chance they were going to do anything with the escape charges. We knew that we had to fight and fight hard against the original convictions, of which he was innocent.

I became a detective, Mike became a paralegal, and we moved mountains. We worked desperately hard, and believe me, trying to gather evidence on a case that is so old isn't easy. The authorities are incredibly hesitant and suspicious. They don't want to tell you anything. In fact, I had to go to great lengths to gather data.

At any rate, we were able to gather enough information and evidence in the case, and we won. Well, in 1991, as Barry just said, we had three first-degree murders that Michael was innocent of overturned by the federal district court as unconstitutional.

This is the only successful inmate *pro se habeas corpus* in the state of Alabama. Of that, we are proud.

Again, we thought we were on our way home. Again, we were wrong. The state, as Barry just said, the state dropped one murder charge, but re-tried one murder. They had a body and a false confession, and the district attorney's office pulled out all the stops, and the judge in the case — being extremely prosecutorial and a lifelong district attorney — did us no favors in the trial, and we lost.

Michael was re-sentenced to a hundred years. Before that, because the three murders have been overturned, the escape charges had been dropped. Now, having been re-sentenced on the one murder, the State of Alabama had the opportunity to re-sentence on the escape charges. They just did that about eight weeks ago.

We had been hopeful that in light of everything that we had done and the time that Mike had spent in prison and the fact he had been such an excellent, excellent inmate and had tremendous commendations — he has a letter from the governor, and there are people in the Department of Corrections who are actually behind Michael. We thought, 'Well, perhaps, today we'll have a break; today the State of Alabama will do something for us.' And then they re-sentenced on his escape charges, life without parole.

So, at this point, we know without a doubt that the State of Alabama is determined to see Michael Pardue die in prison. He is innocent, and we have a mountain of evidence to prove it. They simply will not admit it. They will not see it. I have written scores of letters, made dozens of phone calls, and said, "Please, give me fifteen minutes of your time and I will prove it to you." My phone calls are never returned and my letters are never answered.

Although we are greatly disappointed, we are discouraged, we will continue the fight. We are motivated by two things: primarily our love, because it is profound, and secondly, because we know we are right. Michael Pardue is innocent, and we hold on to the premise that sooner or later, somewhere down the road — and it's a long, long road — truth and justice will prevail, and we pray to God that that's so.

Michael, from his prison cell, wants to thank the organizers of the conference for inviting us so that we could tell our story.

We thank you.

There Is More to Intelligence Than IQ

Stephen Greenspan

INTRODUCTION

A key question that keeps coming up in discussions of Richard Lapointe is: "Why would he confess to a capital crime if he is as innocent as his supporters claim, especially given that his IQ isn't low enough to qualify him for the label mentally retarded?"

I shall attempt to answer this question by discussing what I know about him, about the serious brain disorder of Dandy-Walker Malformation, and about the meaning and limitations of measures of intelligence. I shall speak particularly about *social intelligence*, an aspect of functioning in which Richard is particularly deficient, and explain why a person of limited social intelligence — even when innocent — is vulnerable to confessing under the stresses and challenges of a police interrogation session.

RICHARD LAPOINTE AS A PERSON

My knowledge of Richard comes from having observed him during the trial, from several visits with him in jail, and from interviews with several of the people who have known him during his life.

The first thing to understand about Richard is that he is a survivor. He was born with a brain that is missing a large portion of the *vermis* (or middle section) of the cerebellum, a part of the brain that is involved not only in balance and motor coordination (areas in which he has problems) but which we now understand is involved in higher-order cognitive processes as well.

If you could see a picture of a brain with Dandy-Walker Malformation, you would be struck by how different it looks from a normal brain. It is for this reason that neurologists tend to assume that everyone with Dandy-Walker Malformation has mental retardation (something that is typically, but not always, the case).

In addition to missing a chunk of the cerebellum, people with Dandy-Walker also have a cyst at the opening of the fourth ventricle, partially blocking the draining of cerebrospinal fluid. The result is hydrocephalus, or buildup of fluid, which in most cases, as in Richard's, has to be shunted.

Congenital hydrocephalus is in itself a damaging condition which results in considerable destruction of white matter in the brain, and which creates problems in learning and social functioning, as described in recent work by Jack Fletcher at the University of Texas Medical School in Houston. It was complicated in Richard's case by four additional brain surgeries needed to deal with complications of the original shunt (and at the time his initial shunts were implanted, such surgery was often quite invasive). People with shunted hydrocephalus have a very high likelihood of having what Byron Rourke of Windsor University (in Ontario, Canada) and the Yale Child Study Center calls "nonverbal learning disabilities" (NLD). Among the features of people with NLD are extreme deficits in math calculating ability and in social intelligence (both of which are true of Richard Lapointe).

In Richard's case, the difficulties associated with Dandy-Walker Malformation and hydrocephalus were compounded by the fact that his disability was not diagnosed and treated until he was about 15. He did not receive the special education or other intervention services that he needed. He did not learn in school, and he was held back at least four times, reaching the age of 19 when he dropped out in the ninth grade.

As might be expected, Richard has a number of impairments associated with Dandy-Walker. He cannot do simple math calculations (when serving as a bartender at church functions, he was not allowed to make change as he would hopelessly mess up the cash

STEPHEN GREENSPAN, *Associate Professor of Educational Psychology at the University of Connecticut and President of the Academy on Mental Retardation, is an expert on "social intelligence" who attended Lapointe's trial and has deeply researched the complexities of his mental impairments.*

register). He wears very thick glasses and has poor vision. He wears hearing aids in both ears, and they do not work very well. As a result, he is constantly asking people to repeat themselves, or else makes believe he understands things he did not fully hear or understand. As might be expected with someone missing a portion of his cerebellum, he is awkward and uncoordinated physically, and is often in pain and discomfort from the shunt.

Stephen Greenspan.

As a result of not being diagnosed until so late, Richard adopted a style of survival that was based on covering up his deficiencies (as is true of many people with serious neurological conditions). He is quick to give people what he thinks they want rather than admit that he does not understand something. This was evident to me during his testimony, when the judge once interrupted to advise him that he did not have to agree with everything the prosecutor asked him under cross-examination. This impression was strengthened during a recent interview, when he proved highly suggestible and willing to change a story in order to conform to the pressures and expectations of the examiner.

Another survival tactic of Richard's is his very humorous way of interacting with people (although he did not understand the importance of showing this side of his personality to the jury, and appeared unsmiling and distracted during the trial). He is a very friendly person who is always cracking jokes. Mostly they are corny jokes that are self-deprecating. Drawing on his penchant for rote repetition, he tells these jokes endlessly, no matter that you have heard them dozens of times and no matter how inappropriate they might be. Strikingly, he cannot understand jokes that you tell him, even children's cartoons. This is in line with his social intelligence limitations, particularly his inability to understand novel and ambiguous aspects of situations.

Another characteristic that enabled Richard to triumph over his severe disability is a tremendous work ethic. He is a very hard worker, always trudging off early in the morning to his dishwashing job. He even did so the morning after he returned home from his nine-hour interrogation and confession, going to work even with only three hours sleep and in the upset state that he must have been in.

What one needs to understand about Richard Lapointe is that he deeply cares about people and wants nothing more than to be normal. He loved his life in Manchester, and he loved his wife and child. He was proud of having a job and being able to support his family. He was crazy about his son and loved being a father. He is, in short, a remarkable person, who functioned normally in the community, in spite of having a very significant and debilitating congenital brain disorder.

SOCIAL INTELLIGENCE DEFICITS

I have written quite a bit about a model of social competence, having three components: temperament, character, and social intelligence. *Temperament* has to do with how stable one is emotionally. *Character* has to do with whether one is a nice person who follows rules and cares about others. *Social intelligence* has to do with how "savvy" one is in social situations — that is, with how able one is to figure out what others are thinking or feeling, to understand and/or appreciate the significance of social situations, and to anticipate accurately the consequences of one's actions.

My colleague John Driscoll and I had Richard rated by several people who know him well. The results are quite interesting. Richard is seen as someone with good temperament and character, but with very deficient social intelligence. His temperament and character pattern explain why he was able to triumph to the extent he did over his disability. Such a pattern is consistent with the picture of someone who is a reliable, law-abiding and hard-working person, but very inconsistent with the picture of a brutal murderer.

Congruent with the intellectual limitations associated with Dandy-Walker is Richard's very low social intelligence. It is his low social intelligence that is also responsible for many people's perception of Richard as mentally retarded. This is because in everyday life we think of someone as normal or deficient not on the basis of their academic skills, but on the basis of how they interact with us. And Richard has real limitations in his ability to understand how to deal with certain kinds of social situations.

Examples of Richard being viewed as mentally retarded came during the trial, when a Rehabilitation Services worker defended the fact that she had noted a diagnosis of "mild mental retardation" on a chart by stating that she knew many people with mental retardation and Richard came across to her as such a person. A constant refrain among people who know Richard is that they are surprised his IQ is as high as it is, because he has always behaved — especially in social matters — in a much more limited manner.

According to Maureen Dennis of the Hospital for Sick Children in Toronto, who is one of the few researchers in the world currently carrying out a major study of persons with Dandy-Walker syndrome, people with this disorder demonstrate a great deal of difficulty cognitively processing social information. This is because the cerebellum is very important for making inferences about novel and ambiguous situations. Social situations, I need hardly point out, are often both novel and ambiguous.

Byron Rourke has also made the point that persons with shunted hydrocephalus, especially with right-brain lesions, have similar social limitations. (There was testimony at the trial of "unilateral left-side neglect," a symptom of right-brain lesion, although there is ample other neurological support for the idea that Richard's social limitations are related to Dandy-Walker.) As noted, people with hydrocephalus are at very high risk for nonverbal learning disabilities, which would explain why Richard is competent in relatively ritualized social and work tasks, but less competent in more novel and complex social situations.

Richard's social intelligence limitations were noted at the trial. For example, two employees of the Department of Corrections, a social worker and a psychiatrist, both testified about their concern that Richard was at risk of being victimized by other inmates. Much of this concern stemmed from his inability to figure out the social norms and expectations of prison life. One example of social ineptitude, noted by one of his visitors, occurred when he politely (but very inappropriately) told a deputy warden that he shouldn't be smoking in an area with a no smoking sign (and then failed to understand why the prison official glared at him).

I have collected many stories from Richard's life, including his childhood, of how his low social intelligence would allow him to be manipulated by others. One example that is very relevant to his confession occurred when other kids in his neighborhood talked him into confessing to setting a dumpster on fire, even though he was not actually involved in doing the deed.

It is very possible that Richard's socially inept behavior contributed to his becoming a suspect in the first place. Richard tends to perseverate in his small talk, and it is reported that he constantly brought up the Bernice Martin case whenever Manchester police officers came into the restaurant where he worked as a dishwasher. Being egocentric and lacking perspective-taking skills, Richard would be unlikely to understand that some police officers could view such behavior with great suspicion.

Another aspect of Richard's social intelligence deficit that is relevant to this case is his inability to keep secrets. Many examples were given of how he failed to understand how or why he should keep secrets. Few people who know him believe that if he had murdered Bernice Martin, he could have kept it a secret for two hours, let alone two years.

THE CONSTRUCT OF INTELLIGENCE

A problem in this case is that the prosecution, during the trial and in recent press statements, has pointed to Richard's IQ of 92 as evidence that his confession was competently given. I believe I have already given ample evidence for why I — and all of the eminent clinicians and researchers I have consulted — believe his Dandy-Walker alone should have been sufficient grounds for suppressing the confessions, independent of IQ. However, there is such a fixation on IQ score in this country (as reflected in questions at a news conference the other day) that I feel the need to talk a little bit about intelligence and IQ.

All current tests of IQ are derived from a test that was invented by Alfred Binet and Théodore Simon in France in 1905. Binet and Simon were interested in intelligence much more broadly defined, but were asked by the French government to come up with an instrument which could help to identify school children at risk of failure. To do this, they devised a test that was heavily comprised of items taken from the school curriculum at different ages. As a result, the test they devised (which current IQ tests are heavily based upon) is geared primarily to what Robert Sternberg of Yale terms "academic intelligence" (or what Howard Gardner of Harvard terms "logico-mathematical" intelligence).

Binet and Simon freely acknowledged that they were not tapping all aspects of intelligence in their test. The same admission was made by David Wechsler, the inventor of the most widely used American IQ test. As early as 1920, E.L. Thorndike developed a model of "multiple intelligences" that included three components: *conceptual intelligence* (Sternberg's academic intelligence), *practical intelligence*, and *social intelligence*. The first part is what is tapped by IQ tests. But Thorndike and more recent intelligence theorists such as J.P. Guilford, Sternberg, and Gardner have all argued that one can be normal in IQ (or academic intelligence) while having deficiencies in other areas of intelligence. The opposite, of course, is true as well.

Such variability among and within areas of intelligence is especially true of people with brain insults, where the specific nature of the lesion may affect intelligence in some functional areas while leaving intact functioning in other areas. Gardner's interest in multiple intelligences grew out of his work with brain-injured patients at a VA hospital and his observation about the "modular" nature of intelligence, in which areas of deficit can coexists with areas of normality and even great talent — as in the case of savant skills in people with autism.

Unfortunately, measures of other aspects of intelligence are not widely used or available, so there has been a tendency to inflate the importance of, and to over-rely on, the IQ index — even in situations (such as the social situation of an interrogation) in which it may not be fully relevant. Low IQ has also been used throughout much of this century to institutionalize many thousands of people who had normal social and practical intelligence (as reflected by their good adjustment in society after they were deinstitutionalized). The Lapointe case reflects an opposite example of this phenomenon: someone who has always demonstrated social intelligence deficit in everyday life but who is deemed normal for legal purposes because his IQ (i.e., academic intelligence) score is above some arbitrary ceiling.

Even with respect to academic intelligence, Richard has always functioned in a manner much more impaired than his IQ would suggest he should. This is what we expect from someone missing a chunk of his brain and who suffered the irreversible effects of chronic hydrocephalus. The category of Learning Disabilities was first invented in the 1960s specifically to account for persons who demonstrated relatively normal intelligence but performed poorly in some aspect of academics. The theoretical explanation for this has been that such persons have suffered minimal or more severe brain damage, which affects cognitive functioning in complex ways that are not adequately described by overall IQ score. There has even been recent interest in creating a subcategory of learning disability in which the primary deficit is in social intelligence.

IQ score can be useful in understanding why a person functions as he or she does, but should not be used in itself as evidence of *how* a person functions. Thus, the best evidence that Richard is limited in his ability to understand social situations is that everyone who knows him can give many examples of socially unintelligent behavior on his part. That, and the overwhelming evidence of serious brain damage, should not be dismissed as irrelevant because of a number attained on a test of academic intelligence.

Concepts of Disability

As someone who has been deeply involved over the past several years in efforts to redefine mental retardation and other developmental disorders, I am struck by the inappropriateness of the assumption that these are clear-cut conditions that one either *has* or *does not have*, based on some single criterion such as IQ. In fact, there is much current turmoil over the meaning of mental retardation, learning disabilities, and other disorders (even including schizophrenia), and matters aren't as simple as they are depicted. Unlike physical diseases, where there are specific biological markers, in the field of developmental disorders we often lack objective criteria or standards for saying a person has a particular disorder. This explains the overreliance on IQ, because it is one of the few objective indices we have, and thus it is used even in situations where its use may not be fully relevant and/or may actually be misleading.

Criteria for defining various disabilities are not etched in stone and change periodically. Thus, the IQ cutoff score for mental retardation was raised recently from 70 to 75 (more than doubling the number eligible for services), a decision that was made as much for political as for scientific purposes. There are many, including myself, who argue that IQ is not all that relevant to diagnosing mental retardation, and I have even argued that how one functions in the world should be the main criterion used.

However, it is not necessary to argue that Richard has mental retardation in order to argue that his confessions should have been suppressed. The category of "developmental disabilities" is often used to refer to people who (typically because of a neurological disorder) function as seriously impaired, even when IQ is above the maximum score for diagnosing mental retardation. Autism is a good example of a developmental disability in which one may not have mental retardation (about a third of persons with autism do not, about the same percentage as in Dandy-Walker) but still function with very extreme deficits in social intelligence. (Social intelligence is in fact now recognized as the core deficit in autism, and my colleague Diane Twachtman has noted that Richard's social-processing limitations are similar to those found in persons with high-functioning autism.) In fact, the cerebellar abnormalities in Dandy-Walker are not dissimilar to the kinds of cerebellar abnormalities found in persons with autism by researchers such as Margaret Bauman of Harvard University and Howard Courshesme of the University of California at San Diego.

Would the State be arguing that a person with autism is capable of giving a valid confession just because his or her IQ is above 75? I doubt it. Why? Because it is well-understood that there are severe social limitations which are part and parcel of having autism, and that to ignore these limitations is grossly unfair. One could only speculate on what the outcome in this case would have been if a similar degree of understanding had been demonstrated with respect to the serious disorder known as Dandy-Walker Malformation.

SOCIAL INTELLIGENCE DEMANDS OF INTERROGATION

It is my contention that social intelligence is a skill that is necessary to "survive" a police interrogation. Because certain categories of persons — such as children, persons with mental retardation, and persons with other developmental disorders — demonstrate considerable naivete in their everyday behavior, they should not be subjected to manipulative interrogation techniques.

Obviously, personality factors (such as suggestibility) studied by such scholars as Richard Ofshe in the U.S. and Gisli Gudjonsson in England are powerful determinants of false confession as well. Richard may, thus, be considered *doubly* at risk for false confession, as his social intelligence limitations are combined with a dependent and compliant personality style (he was diagnosed by a psychiatrist as having a Dependent Personality Disorder) associated with false confessions in persons of normal social intelligence.

What are the aspects of a police interrogation that require social intelligence and which a person with social intelligence limitations would have difficulty dealing with? In looking over the literature on interrogation, including the interrogation transcripts of several notorious false confessions, I think the most critical skills needed for an innocent person to come through unscathed are (a) an ability to see through deceptive statements and threats, and (b) an ability to understand accurately the true intentions of the interrogator(s). Of course, it should be noted that the innocent person should also possess sufficient personality strength, as social intelligence alone will not protect him or her from confessing in inquisitorial circumstances.

It is well known that lying is an integral part of police interrogation, and is commonly used to reduce inhibitions in suspects. Confessing, even in the case of deception, is interpreted by law enforcement officers as evidence of a guilty conscience. Yet there are many instances of innocent persons being induced to confess by such tactics.

What are the lies that were told to Richard Lapointe (and to other false confessors such as Peter Reilly), and how is confessing affected by failure to understand such lies?

1. Richard was called in initially on a false pretext. He was told that the police wanted his help in finding the killer. Such a statement must have appealed to his need to feel competent and played into his general desire to be helpful. Thus, it may have been difficult for him to fully comprehend the fact that the situation had shifted and that he was really a suspect in the case, even after he was read the Miranda statement (a statement which Thomas

Grisso has shown to be somewhat difficult to understand).

2. Richard was told that considerable physical evidence existed linking him to the crime. This was in fact con-
cocted, but may have contributed to the development of
a feeling of being trapped and helpless.

3. Richard was apparently told that he could go home once
he confessed. That highly unlikely thing *did* in fact happen. Nevertheless, even if not a literal lie, such a statement was misleading, since he was arrested the next day.
Thus, one deception may have been a general effort to
downplay the importance of confessing. Higher social
intelligence would undoubtedly have enabled Richard
to understand that the short-term advantage of confessing (making police officers happy and getting to go home)
was a zillionfold outweighed by the actual long-term
consequences of confessing.

4. One of Richard's confessions contains words along the
lines of "I must have blacked out" as an explanation for
why he had no memory of the act. I see this phrase all
too often in false confessions (as in Peter Reilly's), and
the most likely explanation is that police tell suspects
this very thing to induce them to confess. (Peter Reilly
was willing to believe this because he was given phony
polygraph results suggesting that he was lying in assert-
ing his innocence.) Higher social intelligence and knowledge of internal psychological process (what Daniel
Goleman, in a recent best-seller, termed "emotional intelligence") would have helped Richard and other false
confessors to avoid falling for such a ploy.

5. False threats are often used, typically late in an interrogation when suspects are exhausted and dispirited (despite the fact that confessors are routinely made to sign
a statement that their confession was not given under
threat). In the case of Peter Reilly, the threat was to throw
him in a dark corner of a jail where he would be brutal-
ized (through maltreatment by other inmates, it was
implied). Johnny Lee Wilson, a Missouri man with mild

mental retardation, confessed — to a crime later admitted by another man — only after he was told that his execution would be sought unless he confessed. (His interrogation, like Peter Reilly's, was taped.) According to Richard (and supported by a transcript of the interrogation of Karen Lapointe by the same police officer), the threat made to him was to have his wife put in jail and his child taken away by welfare authorities.

I have done a great deal of work with parents who have disabilities, and I can tell you that fear of having their child removed is something never far from their consciousness — and is all too often a reality. Richard told Kenneth Selig, a forensic psychiatrist, that the threat to have his child removed "scared the shit out of me" and caused him to cave in and to begin giving the police whatever they wanted.

If Richard had possessed sufficient social intelligence, he would have understood that the officer making this threat did not have the authority to have his child removed. He would have understood that it was a ploy, motivated by desire to secure a confession. He would have understood that the opposite was, in fact, the case: that following his arrest the next day, he would never lay eyes on his son again.

As a parent myself, I know that nothing would be more likely to cause me to sign a confession more quickly than a realistic threat to the well-being of one of my children. The key to whether one could resist such a threat (made more difficult by the exhaustion, terror, isolation and sensory deprivation one experiences in a prolonged interrogation) is one's ability to evaluate the intentions of the threatener and the likelihood of carrying out such a threat. In the case of one of normal social intelligence, it is likely that a threat such as the one allegedly made to Richard would have been discounted as highly implausible. Unfortunately for Richard, normal social intelligence in non-routine situations is not something which he typically demonstrates.

FACTORS CONTRIBUTING TO FALSE CONFESSION

Many researchers, including Professor Gudjonsson in England and Professor Ofshe in the United States, have demonstrated that one does not have to be mentally retarded to succumb to the ploys and deceptions used in interrogation sessions. There is a long literature, including the book by Joost Meerloo entitled *The Rape of the Mind* (about the ordeal of American POWs in Korea), in which it is demonstrated over and over again that some innocent people, even with above-average intelligence, will cave in under the pressures of an inquisitorial interrogation. Gudjonsson has demonstrated, however, that lower intelligence is a factor which increases one's vulnerability to falsely confessing. He found, in fact, that just slightly depressed academic intelligence (below, say, 90 — or about where Richard Lapointe is at) will considerably increase one's likelihood of falsely confessing. Thus, even apart from the very extreme problems associated with Dandy-Walker, one could argue that mental retardation is not necessary to show why Lapointe might be naive enough to give a false confession.

The broader question, therefore, is not whether one is a "disabled confessor" but rather whether one is a "naive confessor." A *naive confessor* may be defined as someone who, in spite of factual innocence, is a "sitting duck" for coercive interrogation techniques. At least three factors contribute to being a naive confessor:

1. personality factors such as a highly compliant and suggestible style,
2. experiential factors such as ignorance of the criminal justice system and lack of understanding of one's legal rights and options, and
3. social intelligence factors such as a relative inability to evaluate the intentions, plausibility and danger of threats, promises and deceptions used to manipulate suspects psychologically in interrogation sessions.

All three of these factors certainly apply to Richard Lapointe and cause him to be eligible for the descriptor "naive confessor":

1. he is a highly suggestible person, as reflected in a diagnosis of Dependent Personality Disorder and our finding that he scored very poorly on Gudjonsson's suggestibility scale;
2. he possessed little understanding of his rights within the criminal justice system, and his only experience with police officers, including some of those who interrogated him, had been one of trust and friendship; and
3. he obviously possessed low social intelligence, as reflected in a lifelong pattern of social ineptness and the symptoms of nonverbal learning disability associated with congenital hydrocephalus and cerebellar malformation.

Persons with particular disability labels, such as brain injury, are at increased risk of having at least one (more typically, at least two) of these characteristics, thereby explaining why persons with particular disability labels are more vulnerable to being naive confessors. Thus, one with a chronic mental illness, such as schizophrenia, probably lacks the personality strength to continue to assert his or her innocence in an interrogation session (and often lacks the social intelligence to see through the manipulative aspects of the session); a person with a condition such as hydrocephalus most likely lacks the social intelligence (and often lacks the personality strength) to deal with such a situation successfully.

One of the most powerful reasons for requiring electronic recording of interrogation sessions is that it provides prosecutors, judges and juries with a reliable direct basis for judging whether a particular confession is or is not given naively, without resorting to the indirect route of *inferring* naivete by looking at the person and his or her limitations outside of the specific context of the interrogation. Thus, in the Peter Reilly case, it should have been obvious to any objective and fair listener (as it was to the judge who overturned his conviction) that Reilly was a naive confessor.

While electronic recording of Richard's interrogation session would have provided objective evidence of the unfairness and invalidity of his confessions, I believe that police also need to develop clearer ethical guidelines regarding the limits of what is permissible in obtaining confessions, especially when dealing with persons known or believed to be naive and socially unintelligent.

Police officers in Manchester knew Richard well, and knew of his reputation as a slow and socially unsophisticated person. They should have acted on that knowledge to guard against his exploitation. Instead, they engaged in a form of "gang mind rape," in which three different police officers — none with any witnesses — proceeded to extract bogus confessions from this exhausted, confused and broken man.

It is not enough to suggest (as was done by one very honorable and fair police officer) that it is up to the courts and not the police to determine whether interrogation practices are proper in a given case. Police interrogators should act fairly and honestly in interrogating suspects, not just because a case might be thrown out by a judge, but because we should not have to imagine any other way for police officers to act.

Securing a false confession just to close a case is doubly horrendous, both in the cost to the innocent confessor and his loved ones, and in the cost to society of allowing an *actual* perpetrator to escape punishment. Saying it is the responsibility of the courts but not of the police to judge the rightness of interrogation tactics is wrong both because it absolves the police of any need to control their own profession, and also because we know from many cases, including Richard's, that judges and juries do not always make correct decisions. Furthermore, without the objective evidence provided by taping, it is difficult for anyone (including police departments wishing to control the behavior of their own officers) to know what actually occurred in a given situation.

Confessions are so powerful that they are difficult to argue against. Police need to understand that their techniques can and sometimes *do* result in innocent but naive persons confessing and suffering the direst and most unjust of consequences. There is a tendency to assume that only the most obviously impaired persons would be so "dumb" as to confess to capital crimes of which they are innocent, no matter how manipulative the techniques they were exposed to. Such an argument is wrong. It is a proven fact, illustrated in several of the cases discussed at this forum, that people with less obvious impairments, like Richard, do often succumb to manipulative interrogation methods. The tragedy of the Richard Lapointe case is that the qualities that made it possible for him to largely overcome his very significant disability also blinded us to his vulnerability to unjust and unfair treatment.

Discussants

[DONALD CONNERY:]
Professor Greenspan has just told us of the police threat to Richard Lapointe to take away his wife and son if he refused to confess.

Even in the absence of a record, we can be confident that Richard spoke truthfully about this part of his interrogation because of the accidental revelation, two years later, of an undisclosed audiotape of the simultaneous police interview with Mrs. Lapointe. When this tape was played in the courtroom, one of the persons listening was a noted Connecticut psychologist, Dr. John Nolte. He has since been dedicated to correcting the Lapointe injustice.

I want to ask Dr. Nolte this: After hearing the questioning of Karen Lapointe, you went home and spent many hours writing a blistering account of this kind of police behavior — which you then widely distributed. What was it that got you so aroused?

[JOHN NOLTE:]
This morning, Professor Ofshe told us that interrogations are stressful, incredibly stressful. This particular interrogation of Karen Lapointe (supposedly an interview) was abusive, incredibly abusive. It begins with the detective going to the Lapointe home, knowing that Richard is at the police station being interrogated himself. With minimal amenities, detective Michael Morrissey says to the wife, "We know who killed your grandmother, it's your husband, Richard."

This is a prevarication. Can you imagine what you would feel if a police detective came to your home and told you that your spouse had committed a heinous murder? It's an emotional blow.

He then goes ahead to lay a claim to world-class dissemination. He says, "I'm trying to help the guy." He and his partner, talking to Richard at the station, are trying to kill Richard Lapointe in the electric chair. He says, "I'm here to find out why; if we know why, we can help him, mitigating circumstances. I'm here to help the guy. Did he have a nervous breakdown? What's this all about?"

Then he adds a little bit of injury to insult. He says, "I have a feeling that you have suspected this all along." Well, Mrs. Lapointe was stunned with that first announcement. She didn't know what to say, particularly because she knew that Richard had not done it. He was at home with her at the time the murder occurred, and I'm sure she was in a state that the psychologists call *cognitive dissonance*. That's when we have two contradictory facts facing us — the contradictory facts being that she knew from her own experience that her husband was in the house with her, and the other fact being that the police are saying, "We have proof; we know that he killed her."

She doesn't quite know what to say, but when he says, "I suspect you have had those suspicions all along, haven't you?," she says no. "Not the slightest?" She says, "Not the slightest."

He tells her a number of things. First of all, he asks her to re-count the events, and when she does, he questions her statement about the family visit. She and the family had been at the grandmother's house earlier in the day that Mrs. Martin was killed, and she says, "We came home together about four o'clock." And he says, "Some of the neighbors say they don't think Richard came home with you."

She says, "Yes, he did; of course he did." Later on, he says, "Some of the neighbors saw Richard take some food to her after dinner." And she says, "No, he didn't leave the house. He didn't leave the house. It never happened." The detective says, "Richard says it did."

This gets her quite confused again. What the heck is she supposed to believe? But she sticks to her story and says, "None of us were going up there," and "None of us had gone up."

Well, she, of course, is giving Richard a solid alibi, and this guy is out to break it down. What he needs to do is to shake her story about Richard leaving the house, so he shifts tactics a little bit. He says, "Now, you told us earlier, the early investigations, that Richard was type O blood. Why did you say that?"

She says, "That's what his mother told me." The cop says, "You misled the investigation. He is type A blood and you know we found some type A blood there that didn't belong to Mrs. Martin. You have misled the investigation." She apologizes and says she is sorry, she didn't mean to, and he says, "You know Richard. What could have caused this to happen?"

She says, "I don't know." He says, "You do know; you have information in your head, and if you don't come forth with it, it's going to bury Richard. You better tell us."

She tries to discuss some of the problems Richard had as a child, and he asks, "Has Richard ever struck your son?" She says, "Never," and nearly comes out of the chair on this one, because she knows that he never, never laid a hand on him, never spanked him, or did any harm to her.

The detective decides to get tough and he says, "Well, you know, we have got to look at this issue of custody of your son, because Richard, he can be arrested because you hindered this prosecution." Essentially, he says to her, "Richard is telling us what really happened. Both of you, there are problems with the statements both of you made before, and Richard is coming clean now and you better come clean, too, and your statements had better match Richard's or it's going to be real trouble for both of you." She, of course, has no idea what Richard is saying at police headquarters.

The detective says, "He said he went back to Mrs. Martin's that night," and she is almost sure it isn't true, so she is in a real bind. She doesn't quite know what to say.

Finally, he says, "Well, you seem to have taken everything I have said in stride. I get the impression you're not surprised at all at anything I have said."

She says, "I *am*. I'm trying not to be too — I mean, I don't want to get sick because I can when I get upset." She does have a chronic disease that makes her susceptible, I believe, to emotional distress. She says, "I don't need that. My son doesn't need it. I know it doesn't seem like I'm upset but I am."

Well, how does he respond to that kind of plea on her part?. Very emphatically, he says, "Well, now, that was a Sunday that day," meaning the day Mrs. Martin was killed.

Well, the interview doesn't go on much longer. He says, "We'll take a statement here." He writes down the statement — if I had more time I would read it to you because it sounds like a policeman making a statement — and he reads it to her and he says, "Is that right?"

She says, "Yes," and he asked her to sign.

He lied to her — lies that were intended to cause emotional distress. He intimidated her. He tried to coerce her into changing her testimony and he threatened her with arrest and the loss of her son. There were no jackboots and instruments of torture; they didn't wave any weapons; but that comes awfully close to police terrorism, I think, and certainly, emotional rape.

An interesting thing: He says to her, he wants to know at one point, "Who can take care of your son if that became necessary?" She says, "Well, my mother and my brother," and she says, "Maybe I should call them," and he says, "No. I wouldn't do that if I were you. We'll know if it's necessary later on, you can call them, but we don't need to get anybody else upset."

Do you know what an adult sexual abuser says to his victim when they part? Don't tell your mother.

Now, the most interesting thing about the whole thing is the existence of this tape. This tape was made and then inadvertently not erased. It was not made to have a record. The reason this tape was made was because a male officer was going into an apartment where he knew there was a single female. The tape — the interview was listened to, was monitored and recorded, so that there was no possibility that this woman could claim an improper advance on the part of the officer later.

This tape was made to protect the officer from this woman.

Well, I was angry, and I'm still angry. But there is another thing Arthur Miller referred to this morning that other people believe, too, and that has to do with the police. We can't simply be angry at them because they do what we ask them to do, and for years, we have had politicians telling us about crime and criminals and they have been encouraging us to ask the police to protect us, and protect us from a certain segment of our society. The police have done their best to try to do it, and sometimes, they lose their moral balance or ethical guidance, and I think this is what happened here.

[CONNERY:]

A pivotal moment in this story came in February 1993 when *The Hartford Courant*'s magazine section published Tom Condon's long investigative report of the Bernice Martin murder case and the selection of Richard Lapointe as a suspect.

Tom is an attorney as well as a veteran journalist and a regular *Courant* columnist. He wrote a column in 1992, following the jury verdict, strongly indicating that an innocent man had been found guilty. Half a year later, his superbly detailed magazine piece made it plain that a terrible injustice had occurred. It should have caused any number of people in the law to raise questions, examine the case and demand an accounting from the prosecutors — but all was silence.

Let me ask you this, Tom: during the trial, what was it that made you think that a miscarriage of justice was underway?

[TOM CONDON:]
Well, I think The Court of Last Resort lives. I got interested because the case itself was starting to draw interest. I heard from Bob Perske and Peg Dignoti. I also heard from a couple of lawyers and a court employee, and I think my job exists because of a wonderful if underappreciated part of human nature, that if people see something wrong, they have an urge to tell somebody, and when it's the system doing wrong, that tends to be us [the press].

I'm always skeptical. I get a letter every other week probably, three or so a month, from inmates or from advocates of inmates. I've gotten three this month so far. Most of them have a certain sameness: I didn't do it, or I did it but the drugs made me do it. And lately I've been getting them from gang members. They say, How could they convict me? I'm only six credits short of my junior college degree.

I went to the trial. I went up and sat — actually, I didn't know John Nolte at the time, but I went up and sat near him behind Richard, and Richard appeared to be asleep. It then occurred to me that perhaps he wasn't appreciating what was going on around him. As I continued to look into it, it just became preposterous to me that he was on trial at all, that he had been arrested. Distilled to its essence, the case comes down to two questions: Did he do it? Did he get a fair shake?

Did he do it? He had no motive, no opportunity, and I don't believe he had the ability to do it. If you accept Karen Lapointe's four different statements as true, under this tremendous pressure that you have seen, then there was a time frame on the evening of the killing in which Richard Lapointe — bumbling, off-plumb, clumsy Richard Lapointe — had to walk from his house back to Bernice Martin's apartment, about a ten-minute walk, have coffee with her, then commit the act of a raging maniac, then walk back and be sitting there, no marks, no blood, no sweat on him watching TV when Karen came back downstairs. No.

The fact that he was convicted indicates to me that there was a stereotyping of a person with mental handicaps. The idea of someone who could instantaneously lose control, lose everything, turn into a raging maniac, and then turn back again, an hour later — something that had never happened in his life before. But I think too many of us are willing to believe that that will happen, even though there is not a scintilla of evidence that something like that can happen.

Did Richard Lapointe get a fair shake? Come on! You saw in the video [*A Passion for Justice*] that I said he would have confessed to killing Abraham Lincoln. He would have confessed to crucifying Jesus Christ. He had no idea. He was ridiculously overmatched. Talk to the people who know him. He couldn't have kept a secret for two years if he had done this crime, so it was preposterous that he was convicted on the basis of this confession.

Many of you have read my article, and I show that his confession doesn't jibe in almost every salient detail with experts' testimony of how the crime was committed. Detective Morrissey got him to confess to strangling with his hands, but Bernice Martin *wasn't strangled that way*. She was strangled from the side. Richard confessed to having intercourse. But it wasn't intercourse; she was sexually assaulted with a blunt instrument. These are fairly key details.

I don't believe he did it. I don't believe he was afforded due process. It is embarrassing to me that the state won't take a second look. Justice, the judicial system, which is a human institution, can be subject to frailty. Why can't we admit that? The ultimate wrong, the ultimate crime, the ultimate sin here is that the state ruined a heroically happy family.

[CONNERY:]

That's a great phrase, *heroically happy family*, because while Richard Lapointe was no angel, and had his share of faults or annoying habits or whatever else you might want to say about a fellow imperfect human being, he was a success as a husband, a father and a working man. He put together a good life against great odds, and then it was destroyed in the name of the people of Connecticut.

But it also needs to be said that Richard could not have had two finer or more decent and conscientious public defenders if he had looked all over Connecticut or the nation to find them. These gentlemen put their heart and soul into defending him, and you saw in the film earlier in the day how Pat Culligan found it very difficult to express his emotions about not being able to keep this matter from going to a guilty verdict.

I'm going to make two people in this audience very, very unhappy because they've sat here so quietly and they've never sought headlines, but I want to ask Pat Culligan and Chris Cosgrove to please stand up so that we can say thanks to them. [Applause.]

Now, one positive fallout of Tom Condon's article was the impact it had on a number of readers. They wanted to know what they could do to help Richard Lapointe. No two people were more moved to action, and have been more steadfast, than Margene Castle and her husband John, who is a training officer with the Motor Vehicle Department.

John, you are an organizer. You became the coordinator of The Friends of Richard Lapointe and a kind of information center about the case. As a private person, you represent the dozens of so-called average citizens who got involved in this case. Why? Why are the two of you so committed?

[JOHN CASTLE:]
That Sunday in February 1993 was a very, very long day. Margene, my wife, had read Tom Condon's article, and she said, "Oh, we have to get involved. Here, John, read it." I sat down and read it. "Yes, dear, we've got to get involved." She wanted to get hold of Tom Condon right away, but it was a Sunday and I didn't think we'd be able to reach him.

Well, that was a long night for Margene. And the first thing Monday morning, she was on the horn, talking to Tom, asking how could she become involved. He referred her to Pat Beeman in Manchester. She called Pat, and so we became involved, and we are still very much involved.

We see Richard probably every week or so. We talk to him, it seems like, every night. We can't phone him; the call has to come from Richard, collect. I might say as a sideline, it's a dollar and eighty-six cents every time he calls, so if he phones three times in one night, it adds up.

When we started with the group — the people that Bob Perske got together way back during the days of the trial — it was Margene who went regularly. The meetings were held at noontime once a month, and she would talk me into staying instead of just picking her up and taking her home. Basically, people were saying, "What are we going to do for poor Richard?" I began to realize that they were doing things, but they weren't really coming around with any concrete ideas, so we finally were able to get them to meet in the evenings so that at least some of the menfolk could come along and see what was happening. Then there came a time when we had to find another meeting place.

Well, I was aware that the Burger King in Wethersfield has a big meeting room, so I went over and arranged to use the room and it has been our meeting place, every other Wednesday night, ever since. A lot of folks came. We have had about a hundred members but we have averaged about fifteen to twenty members at a meeting, more on special occasions, and that's pretty much what it has been for two and a half years now. Burger King has been extremely generous about this. Some of us get there directly from work, some as early as five o'clock even though things don't get serious until about six. We buy our hamburgers and shakes and take them into the meeting room, and when enough people get there, we start.

It's informal, and I'm not a president, I'm a coordinator. There are a lot of little things that need doing, but our focus is on the big things, such as this forum, which I suppose we can consider our crowning achievement until the day Richard Lapointe walks out of prison as a free citizen once again.

[CONNERY:]
The *Journal Inquirer* of Manchester, the scene of the crime and the Lapointe home, did some very solid reporting of the murder and the court activities. But it was only later that the editors fully realized

that there might have been a wrongful conviction. At that point, they really got into it, and they have run some powerful editorials and columns describing this as one of the worst travesties of justice in Connecticut history.

Alex Wood was assigned to do the major investigation for the paper in late 1994. It turned out to be a long, exquisitely detailed series of articles that exposed any number of instances of police misconduct and prosecution excesses.

I have never known a journalist to go so diligently and deeply into the records and explore the legal issues. What happened, Alex? How did you get into this?

[ALEX WOOD:]
I guess this is an example of why groups like The Friends of Richard Lapointe are important, because my first involvement in this case was just covering on a fill-in basis a few days of the trial, and then I really had nothing more to do with it until a long time later when I was assigned to do a story on The Friends of Richard Lapointe.

I called up some people and talked to them, and so forth, but I also happened to be given the file of documents that a colleague had compiled on the case. I started to look through them, and in the course of doing that, I was very interested in the Michael Morrissey/ Karen Lapointe tape because I had heard some of the testimony relating to that, and there were some things that I wanted to try to sort out in my own mind.

So I read that transcript, and then I read Judge Barry's decision on the motion to suppress. In there, he recites testimony from the detectives and from Richard Lapointe, and at one point, he summarizes Detective Morrissey's testimony. He quotes Morrissey as denying that he had made a threat to Richard Lapointe, a threat that if Richard's story and his wife's didn't match, she could be arrested and their son made a ward of the state. And all of a sudden, a little light went on in my head, and it was like, *Hey, I just read Morrissey doing that — using a threat — in this transcript over here.* Admittedly, in a different interview, but it's on the same night and it's only a few hours apart. That really shook me because, frankly, up until that time, I was pretty comfortable that the case had been accurately resolved.

Perhaps I had been naive, but I just couldn't imagine a police officer testifying other than truthfully on the question of a suspect volunteering information that only the killer would know. So I didn't see any urgency about doing anything about it until that point, but when you start to realize that perhaps Richard Lapointe was the one telling the truth on this point, what else was he the one telling the truth on? And that becomes very disturbing, so I started to look at the details of the case.

Actually, initially, my idea was to just take a couple of vignettes out of the Richard Lapointe case and use that as a taking-off point for an issue piece on whether confessions should be taped and to what extent it is proper for police to use deception. But as I got to know more about the case, it became more and more involved, and I realized that the depth of some of the questions and problems here was a good deal greater than I had thought. So I managed to get hold of transcripts, and what we ended up with was a four-part series on the Richard Lapointe case and then an additional part on the issues as I had originally envisioned.

The one adjective that is always used when people talk about the series I wrote on the case is "long," and that's probably true. I owe a lot to my editors at the *Journal Inquirer* for having let me use as much space as we did on that.

[CONNERY:]
When we planned this forum to draw public attention to the reasons for wrongful conviction, we never thought of ourselves as being *against* police and prosecutors. After all, we need them to keep us safe; we need them to fight crime and do justice. We want to support them. Arthur Miller told you earlier that we should "protect the police, even from themselves," and that we "need their principled upholding of the law."

So it seemed to us only fitting that we should conclude these proceedings with a few words from two extremely experienced officers of the law, both now retired. One is deeply committed to freeing Richard Lapointe; the other, uninvolved in the Lapointe case, is an advocate of the highest possible standards of police work.

First, Andy Lefebvre. He and his wife Florence have been among the most faithful Friends of Richard. Yet he has spent most of his adult life in police work. He was the Detective Division Commander of the Bloomfield, Connecticut, Police Department.

Andy, I have to ask: What's a nice guy like you doing in a crowd like this?

[ANDY LEFEBVRE:]
First of all, I got involved because of Father Dennis Ferrino. He's my pastor at the church. He heard about this injustice and asked me if I would look into it. Of course, the next step was to go to Tom Condon's article, like everybody else did, and I just couldn't believe it.

I did have occasion to see Richard on a couple of occasions. I think the whole case boils down to what they call a detailed confession. I quite frankly don't view it as a confession at all. I view it as an admission, an admission of guilt by somebody else's words.

There's nothing — he adds nothing independently here. I view a confession as giving details of a crime. There were no details of a crime here, and in defense of the police department, which has been getting a little bit too much of a bad rap, I think there are safety gaps, and the safety gaps should have been at the prosecutor's level.

I worked fifteen years in the bureau. I worked with half a dozen prosecutors, and I don't know of any one prosecutor that would have signed a warrant like that if I brought it to him, and that's fifteen years ago, so I certainly don't see why this one was signed.

[CONNERY:]
Finally, George Moore. I admire this man for his willingness to attend this event and offer us his reactions. I would like to think that it is a measure of our own confidence that we are giving him the last word on the big issues we have discussed here today. After all, he, like Andy, has spent most of his adult life in police work — and even now, as the founder and president of his own firm, Moore Technologies, he works around the country as a police consultant. As a Connecticut State Police officer, he became a communications specialist and rose to the high rank of lieutenant colonel, making him one of the top commanders of the force before his recent retirement.

George, what would you like to say?

[GEORGE MOORE:]
The first thing is: I know how General Custer felt when he got the

invitation from Chief Crazy Horse.

All kidding aside, after hearing what's been talked about here I can't help but think back to some other cases that I heard about early in my career. They were cases that brought about Supreme Court decisions. At the time it occurred, the conduct of the police officers was so outlandish that you stood there and said, "What idiot would ever do that?" But somebody did, and I'm not saying that's what happened here, but if you think back, anybody who is familiar with the *Mapp vs. Ohio* decision on searches — those guys had a piece of paper they claimed was a search warrant. They were waving it around, and the woman grabs it and puts it down her dress, so they just reach in and take it back. You can't do that, but the point is: do these things happen? Yes. They grabbed it and took it back. *You can't do that.* But the point being, *do* these things happen? Yes, they do happen.

It is very, very unfortunate that it occurs but, hopefully, we have checks and balances built within our system. The job of the police is to investigate, to gather the facts and establish probable cause. That's the operative word here: *probable cause* to present to the court that the accused committed a crime.

If the prosecutor and the judge agree that there's probable cause, they issue an arrest warrant, and they say, "We believe there's probable cause to try this person for the crime," and so the process begins.

The next step goes to a much higher level which is proof beyond a reasonable doubt, and that's where the whole trial process comes in. And after that, you get to the appeal process and everything else.

Do mistakes happen? Yes, they do, absolutely, but there are so many things I'm hearing here today that I'm saying to myself, "How do you make this work in reality?"

I heard talk before about totally getting rid of plea bargaining, and at the same time I'm hearing that, I'm hearing somebody else saying that every time you have interrogation, you ought to have a lawyer in the room. Well, I sit here and say, well, that's going to work real nice because if there is a lawyer in the room, you're never going to get a confession because the first thing the lawyer is going to tell the guy is, "Don't say a word" — which is the right thing. That's what you're paying lawyers to tell you.

Now, if you're not going to have plea bargaining, the entire criminal justice system is going to collapse under its own weight because we just cannot afford, there's not enough time, there's not enough buildings in the state of Connecticut to have a trial for every time somebody is arrested. It's just a fact of life. Plea bargaining has to occur. There's just no way around that.

The other thing gets into the issue of determining the impact of a person's mental limitations or physical limitations on their ability to be truthful and so forth. I don't know of too many people who wear badges that have the ability to make that determination. In fact, I was reading in the articles here, there aren't many *lawyers* that realize their client doesn't possess that kind of skill. One of the other things, and I forget who it was that said it here, they mentioned that Richard looked like he was asleep during the trial. Well, so does O.J. Simpson, but that's another issue.

I think the big question — and I know that Don [Connery] and I have talked about this — is the issue of videotaping. Should interrogations be taped? And my own personal feeling is as a matter of practicality, yes, they should be. They can't *always* be for any number of reasons. These things don't always occur in a police interrogation facility; there are many times when an interview is going to occur at a place where I just don't have the wherewithal to bring the tape equipment with me.

The real reservation is this: if it becomes a requirement of law and then for some reason you're not able to have the tape, it ends up coming back as one more reason why you're not going to get that confession in.

Having the tape is a double-edged sword — in that it keeps the police honest, but it also becomes very valuable to them in prior inconsistent testimony if the guy ever wants to recant his statement later on. So it's going to come around, okay? And even a false confession, maybe it will get buried in the file someplace for a long time and you will eventually find it, but when these things come out and you start to see I've got three different confessions from this guy confessing to three different things in three different ways, that certainly ought to bring some question as to the credibility of what he finally confessed to. So I think the whole thing is we have to have some faith in the system, and we have to let the system do what it's supposed to do, and let the chips fall where they may.

Under Commissioner [Cleveland] Fuessenich, and I really respected the man, I can remember the first time when the State Police started using videotapes. It was back in the mid-'70s, and we started using videotapes for DWI [Driving While Intoxicated] arrests. It was the greatest thing in the world because you would arrest this guy for DWI, and go through the test process and everything else, and three or four weeks later now you're in court, and they're trying to negotiate something in the prosecutor's office, and here's this nice guy in a three-piece suit standing there with his lawyer, and he looks all super nice until you play the videotape. You show this slobbering drunk rolling around on the floor. Case closed. He ends up pleading guilty.

So for the most part, I would like to think the tapes are going to corroborate the fact. Again, for the most part, I like to think that the police are doing a good job, and I know from my experience that they are trying, they are trying real hard, and I think there was one statement I heard earlier where they referred to the police being *vicious* in trying to get these confessions. I think I would use the term *overzealous*. I would like to think it's a very small percentage of people out there that have badges on their person that would knowingly go out and try to railroad somebody or hang a bad rap on somebody. I just find that very, very difficult to believe.

[ROBERT PERSKE:]
I'm amazed and I'm without words about what has happened here today. I remember walking into that courtroom on May 6th, 1992. I sat behind Richard Lapointe, and he was the most friendless, forsaken guy I ever saw in my life. The state had dehumanized him. They saw him as a non-person — someone who was going to be out of there and headed for the electric chair. So I panicked, and I went to work, and I am amazed at how you can find one person and then another person and another person and then we find more people.

It has taken three years so far. One little secret about me is that I live down in Darien, but I don't live in fancy Darien. I'm right next to the Amtrak trains, so when they go by the dishes rattle. But I'm a romantic and I stand out there and I say as those Amtrak trains go by, "Look at her go! Look at her go!" Somebody stopped me one day and said, "Why do you keep saying that?" And I said, "That's the only thing I don't have to push."

I have to tell you, this gang that's trying to rescue Richard Lapointe has been self-propelled. Everybody is unique and unrepeatable. I'm amazed that we have come such a long way from May 6th, 1992, to this forum. It was going to be a local forum until we started to ask national people, and they all volunteered to come, so then it became a national thing — and you ain't seen nothing yet, folks. We are not going to stop. We are not going to stop.

PART III

REPORTS OF
A QUEST FOR
JUSTICE

FOR MANY, ECHOES OF AN INJUSTICE IN CONNECTICUT

Convicted Slayer's Backers Say His Confession, Like One 20 Years Ago, Was Coerced

By JONATHAN RABINOVITZ

HARTFORD, Sept. 14 — When Peter A. Reilly's conviction for killing his mother was overturned two decades ago, it was a lesson to many in Connecticut and the nation on how the police can abuse the powers of interrogation to elicit a false confession from a naive suspect.

At the time, Mr. Reilly's many supporters, including most notably the playwright Arthur Miller, hoped their efforts on his behalf would put an end to leading questions, sleep deprivation and other coercive tactics that had led to what a state judge declared "a grave injustice."

Now, Mr. Miller and Mr. Reilly, among others, have taken up a new cause, the imprisonment of a brain-damaged man, Richard Lapointe, who supporters say was coerced into confessing to the rape and murder of his wife's grandmother.

"It's the Peter Reilly case all over again," Mr. Miller said today. "I thought we'd learned something from that: that you cannot base a whole case on a confession, especially in the case of a person of the mental capacity of this one."

"I was simply amazed that they could do this again," Mr. Miller said.

Mr. Lapointe, 49, a dishwasher nicknamed Mr. Magoo for his thick glasses, small stature and awkward gait, has undergone brain surgery five times. His supporters describe him as a clumsy man who wears a hearing aid, gets dizzy if he turns too quickly, is not coordinated enough to drive, and tells his visitors at the prison the same knock-knock jokes again and again.

Those who have lined up behind him, including many advocates for the retarded, say he was physically and mentally incapable of committing the brutal stabbing and rape of 88-year-old Bernice Martin on March 8, 1987. They say his confession — the linchpin of a case that lacks any definitive physical evidence linking him to the crime — came in a 10-hour interrogation when the police denied Mr. Lapointe a lawyer, threatened to harm his family and prevented him from going to the bathroom until he admitted his guilt.

To complicate matters, his supporters say, Mr. Lapointe seeks to please authority figures. And while the police recorded an interview with his wife, Karen, they did not record Mr. Lapointe's confession.

As the appeal wends its way to the State Supreme Court, prosecutors have derided Mr. Lapointe's supporters. The Hartford State's Attorney, James E. Thomas, whose office tried the case, pointed out that a judge spent a month holding a hearing on the confession before upholding it, that a jury found Mr. Lapointe guilty and that Mr. Lapointe has scored as high as 92 on an I.Q. test, so he should not be considered retarded.

"It's basically a *cause célèbre*," Mr. Thomas said. "It represents the opinion of a select few that Mr. Lapointe is the so-called wrong man, but they're unable to point to anything substantive to indicate that he is in fact the wrong man."

Mr. Lapointe's wife and members of her family have told reporters that they believe Mr. Lapointe is guilty and have said that he was capable of committing the crime. And one relative complained to a reporter from the *Journal Inquirer* in Manchester, where the crime occurred, that Mr. Lapointe's supporters are needlessly interfering.

But the doubters are persistent. Mr. Miller, Mr. Reilly and Richard Ofshe, a sociology professor who studies coerced confessions, are among those who plan to appear at a symposium on Saturday in Hartford titled "Convicting The Innocent." It was inspired by the Lapointe case.

Their point of view has won support among the local news organizations. *The Hartford Courant* has said in an editorial that "the case cries for re-examination" and it ran a 5,000-word cover story in its Sunday magazine by a columnist and lawyer, Tom Condon, proclaiming Mr. Lapointe's innocence. The *Journal Inquirer* printed a five-part series, "Tainted Justice," that said a review of court documents "raises disturbing questions about the credibility of the police case."

Donald S. Connery, the author of a book on the Reilly case, *Guilty Until Proven Innocent,* said he remains convinced that the Manchester Police Department arrested the wrong man and that once again, the state has sent someone to jail based solely on a weak confession.

Mr. Connery, a former foreign correspondent for *Time* magazine, has joined The Friends of Richard Lapointe, a group that includes teachers, housewives, a retired police detective and a court stenographer, among others, that has met almost every other Wednesday night for the last two years at a Burger King in Wethersfield.

Mr. Connery was pivotal in bringing in Mr. Miller and Mr. Reilly, in helping recruit one of the state's preeminent defense lawyers to handle the case *pro bono*, and in initiating the symposium, which is to have experts from around the nation to talk about false confessions.

On Wednesday afternoon, Mr. Connery was visiting Mr. Reilly to discuss Mr. Reilly's talk. During the visit, he recalled his initial reaction in 1974 when his daughter, a high school classmate of Mr. Reilly's in Litchfield County, Connecticut, urged him to help Mr. Reilly.

"I remember saying, he confessed, he's been arrested, a jury has found him guilty, and besides which, he's in prison," Mr. Connery said. The case seemed closed.

But when Mr. Reilly was released on bond, and Mr. Connery's daughter brought Mr. Reilly to a pool party at their home in Kent, Mr. Connery could not believe that Mr. Reilly, then 19, was guilty.

As Mr. Connery studied the issue, he said that he became aware of "the phenomenon of false confessions."

"It's fascinating how some suspects — even though they know in their heart that they didn't do it — will confess," Mr. Connery said. Mr. Reilly, who experienced 24 hours of interrogation, remarked:

"It becomes a guessing game, as you try to figure out what they want to hear. It's a combination of fatigue and a state of mind that no one in the world could believe this. They keep pushing, and saying maybe you did this, and they suggest things. And then a half-hour later, you pick it up."

At one point in his interrogation, which was taped, Mr. Reilly said, "I think I'm making this up."

Looking back at it, he said, "If they wanted me to say I was at Ford's Theater, I would have said it."

Mr. Lapointe's supporters say that his case is even more egregious than Mr. Reilly's, noting Mr. Lapointe's impairment and the failure of the police to record his interrogation, more than two years after the crime, on July 4, 1989. There was little physical evidence, as a fire had been set in Mrs. Martin's apartment after the killing, and the blood and semen found there reportedly could match 28 percent of the male population.

Accordingly, in court, the recollection of the interrogation became a matter of Mr. Lapointe's word against that of the police. The jury believed the police.

The police deny that they made Mr. Lapointe stay against his will or stopped him from calling a lawyer. "Mr. Lapointe was accorded due process right down the line," said Mr. Thomas, the prosecutor [the current Hartford-area state's attorney, speaking on behalf of colleagues who won the conviction in 1992].

But in analyzing the proceedings, supporters of Mr. Lapointe find conflicts among police testimony, Mr. Lapointe's signed confessions, other witnesses' testimony and Mr. Lapointe's testimony.

For instance, the police said that Mr. Lapointe's final confession has information that only the killer would know — such as Mrs. Martin's having been raped. Yet the *Journal Inquirer* had already reported the victim's sexual assault and acquaintances of Mr. Lapointe had mentioned it.

The most incriminating points in the confession, that Mr. Lapointe knew of a semen stain on the bed and that Mrs. Martin was killed with a kitchen knife, could have been suggested by police or even guessed, Mr. Lapointe's supporters say.

Mr. Lapointe's supporters question whether the police testimony can be trusted, noting that police originally testified that Karen Lapointe's interview was not taped, a falsehood discovered accidentally when the police turned the tapes over to the prosecutor.

In explaining why they think Mr. Lapointe could have been singled out, his supporters say that his disability made him an easy scapegoat.

The Hartford Courant, September 10, 1995

LAPOINTE CASE RAISES TROUBLING QUESTIONS

A Fair Judicial Shake for "Limited" People?

By KATHLEEN MEGAN

Did Richard Lapointe confess to raping and killing his wife's grandmother in an effort to tell police what he sensed they wanted to hear?

Or because he was told that if he confessed he could use the bathroom?

Or because he believed that unless he confessed his wife would be jailed or his son taken away from him?

Or because he actually killed her?

Was he unable because of brain abnormalities to understand the gravity of a confession or to withstand the rigors of a nine-hour interrogation?

Those are some of the unanswered questions of debate in the Lapointe case.

They are questions that will probably never have clear answers because there is no written or taped record of the interrogation that led to his confession on July 4, 1989 — a confession that was largely the reason for his conviction and life sentencing in 1992.

And they are questions that have focused attention not just on the Lapointe case, but on the concerns of all suspects who are mentally retarded or mentally limited in some way.

With more and more mentally retarded people leaving institutions for the community all across the nation, the issue of how to accommodate them if they enter the criminal justice system in the community is growing in importance.

While statistics are not available, experts estimate that people of limited intelligence are no more likely to enter the criminal justice system than their normal peers.

But when they do, according to experts on the subject, they have a much harder time along the judicial trail. They are far more likely to provide a false confession, to misunderstand legal terms such as their Miranda rights, and to be misunderstood by police and legal authorities. They are far more suggestible and more easily intimidated, the experts say, often saying what they think the police officer wants to hear.

They plead guilty more readily than defendants without mental retardation and are more often convicted of the arrested offense rather than a reduced charge. What's more, the experts add, judges, lawyers and others involved in the criminal justice system frequently fail to recognize their limited mental capacity and pre-trial psychological exams are not requested.

And, they are less likely to be considered for probation or other programs that are alternatives to prison. Their convictions are also appealed less frequently.

"The system does not give a fair shake to people with diminished intellects," said Dolores Norley, a Florida lawyer with a mentally retarded adult child who has developed curriculums to familiarize police and court officials with the needs of mentally limited people. "It isn't always deliberate....The attorneys don't understand, and they turn into the judges, and there we are with a system that doesn't understand these people who do not understand."

Suzanne Lustig, a lawyer who is director of a New Jersey program designed to assist in developing "personal justice plans" for people with mental limitations, said, "They are worse off every step of the way" than their normal peers.

IMPROVEMENT

While efforts such as Norley's and Lustig's may be rare, there are many signs that advocates and experts are becoming more aware of the problem and attempting to address it.

In Connecticut, a group of supporters who believes the imprisoned Lapointe is innocent, is fighting to reopen his case, which is under appeal to the state Supreme Court.

Elsewhere, at Miami University in Ohio, Professor Caroline Everington has developed a new testing instrument to determine whether a mentally limited person is competent to stand trial. The usual standard is to determine whether a defendant is capable of understanding the charges against him and whether he is capable of assisting in his defense.

This new test asks multiple choice and open-ended questions, covering topics such as the role of the judge, the role of the lawyers and the consequences of a conviction.

At the University of North Carolina at Chapel Hill, Professor George S. Baroff advocates the use of a simpler version of the Miranda rights, to ease understanding.

"I was on the phone this morning trying to get police to use the modified forum," Baroff said last week.

WHO ARE THEY?

When experts talk about serving people with a limited mental capacity, they say the biggest problem is simply identifying them. Very often, such persons are "very streetwise, knowledgeable. They look like you or me," said Lustig.

"They know they don't get things as quick as someone else does, but they hide it so they aren't going to let on or tell anyone they have a disability."

Often, their lawyers don't even realize they are mentally limited. Lustig recalls one lawyer who thought his client was "a wise guy" until he got his educational records.

Another difficulty in identifying people whose testimony or behavior may be affected by mental limitations is an overreliance on IQ test results. Generally, people with mental retardation have an IQ of 69 or below.

Yet experts say there are different types of intelligence. Stephen Greenspan, an associate professor at the University of Connecticut, said IQ accounts for only academic intelligence.

More important in day-to-day functioning is what he calls "social intelligence." Someone with an IQ of 70 or above, but lacking in social intelligence or understanding, may be unable to fend for themselves when faced with complex and ambiguous situations such as a police interrogation.

When Richard Lapointe scored 92 on an IQ test, that placed him at the low end of normal — well above the cut-off associated with mental retardation.

Greenspan and others said they think that made it difficult for jurors to believe arguments that his brain damage and related physical problems could have rendered him incapable of committing such a crime or would have left him unable to understand the consequences of confessing to the murder of Bernice Martin.

"It is because of his social dumbness rather than his learning difficulties that many people who knew and worked with Lapointe thought of him as a mentally retarded person," Greenspan wrote in a paper. "A constant refrain among people who know Richard Lapointe is that his IQ does not give a valid picture of how he actually functions."

Experts say that how a person functions in ordinary life is a more valid measure of his or her disability than an IQ score.

LISTENING TO AUTHORITIES

The matter of false confessions given by suspects with mental limitations is another major factor in their higher rate of conviction, experts say.

People with a limited mental capacity have often led lonely, isolated lives. They have learned to get along by listening to authorities and doing what they are told.

In their desire to please authorities, make friends and often to bluff a greater degree of competence, they frequently are more suggestible than a normal person would be.

Lustig said that police officers are therefore told to stay away from yes and no questions or questions that begin, "Is it true...." In such cases, mentally limited people are far more likely to respond in whatever manner they think the police officer desires. Better, Lustig said, to ask questions that enable suspects to give their own accounts of what happened.

Greenspan believes an innocent suspect with little social intelligence is particularly ill-prepared to withstand a standard police interrogation.

As manipulative and deceptive techniques are often used in police interrogations, Greenspan said, an innocent person needs "an ability to see through deceptive statements and threats" and an ability to "understand accurately the true intentions of the interrogator."

But in the end, what can be done to ensure that a person with limited mental capacity has a fair trial?

Experts have several recommendations. First, they recommend that a genuine effort be made to ensure that suspects understand the Miranda rights. The typical quick read through the rights does not ensure this, they argue.

Any interrogations or confessions, they say, should be tape-recorded or videotaped so that a jury can later assess its fairness and truth.

They also recommend educational programs for police, lawyers and judges to learn more about how to work with people with a limited mental capacity.

And they recommend that sentencing should take into account recommendations by both mental retardation professionals and corrections experts.

EASY CONFESSIONS MAKE TOUGH LAW

A Convicted Murderer Tries to
Persuade the State Supreme Court
That His 'Dependent Personality'
Made Him Falsely Admit the Crime

By PAUL FRISMAN

A suspect so deferential and compliant when police grill him about a murder that he confirms their suspicions and confesses to the killing: What could be better? It's a cop's dream.

Unless the suspect is innocent, a "naive confessor," the kind of individual who is socially inept, cowed by authority figures, eager to please — someone, his supporters say, like Richard A. Lapointe.

Lapointe, now 49, was convicted in 1992 of murdering his wife's 88-year-old grandmother and sentenced to life in prison without parole. His supporters, including journalists, academics and leading literary lights, say Lapointe was railroaded by a system that ignored his obvious mental shortcomings.

University of Connecticut psychology professor Stephen Greenspan says Lapointe, with a congenital brain malformation and a highly dependent personality, was able to manage in a predictable, routine world. But that world collapsed during a nine-hour police interrogation in the Manchester Police Department.

The confession that Lapointe gave Manchester police during that

PAUL FRISMAN is a reporter for The Connecticut Law Tribune. *This article is published with permission from* The Connecticut Law Tribune, *an American Lawyer Media company, September 18, 1995. ©1995 The Connecticut Law Tribune.*

time is the key to his conviction. Lapointe's supporters say it is a false confession, given by a man unable to cope with police interrogation techniques, ignorant of his legal rights and "abnormally hungry to please authority figures."

Those three factors, Greenspan says, make Lapointe a "naive confessor... a sitting duck for coercive interrogation techniques."

THE IQ TEST

On appeal, New Haven attorney John R. Williams argues that trial testimony shows Lapointe suffers from dependent personality disorder, the symptoms of which include deference to authority, high suggestibility and a tendency to be compliant and submissive.

"The combination of the Manchester Police Department's use of deliberate deception and Mr. Lapointe's impaired personality made a confession almost inevitable, even if the confession was not true," writes Williams, of The Law Offices of John R. Williams, in his appeal brief.

But an attempt to suppress the confession failed because the prosecution, focusing relentlessly on Lapointe's 92 IQ — within the normal range — was able to persuade Superior Court Judge David M. Barry that Lapointe was capable of giving a knowing, voluntary and intelligent confession.

Greenspan, president of the Academy on Mental Retardation, says it's "absurd" to say that because someone "doesn't have mental retardation, therefore he's normal." IQ measures academic achievement, he says, not social or practical skills.

"People at the low end of the spectrum in terms of IQ... could function very well in society," Greenspan says. "The flip side is true. It's possible for somebody to appear normal because of his IQ being above normal [and] still have severe problems in social and practical functioning."

Lapointe, for example, "functioned in the real world as highly manipulatable, highly gullible, susceptible to pressure typical of interrogation," he says. Despite Lapointe's IQ, many people regarded him as retarded because of the way he interacted with them, Greenspan says.

Lapointe didn't help his cause when he tried to hide his deficiencies at trial. "His whole style in life has been to be seen to be smarter than he is," says author Donald Connery, a leader in the effort to reopen Lapointe's case. "He doesn't want to accept that he doesn't know what's happening."

Determining social intelligence poses a problem for lawyers because it's hard to quantify, says Hartford criminal-defense attorney James W. Bergenn, a partner in Shipman & Goodwin. IQ "has a numerical value," he says. "Everybody in America falls for numbers."

Without facts and figures, Bergenn says, the question of competence becomes an argument between experts. "Once you open the door to a bunch of social scientists coming in [to say] where somebody falls in the [intelligence] spectrum, it's mush mind," he says. "It's hard to get your hands on."

THE SUGGESTIBLE SUSPECT

Bergenn is sympathetic to the problem posed by the Lapointe case. He knows the problem firsthand.

As a federal public defender in the early 1980s, Bergenn had a client accused of wrongfully obtaining veterans' benefits. The client told Bergenn at the initial interview that he was innocent.

Bergenn routinely asked if the client had talked to the police. Yes, he had, the client said. What did he tell them? the young lawyer asked. "I told them I did it," his client said.

And why was that, asked Bergenn, somewhat taken aback. "Because I failed the lie detector test," his client said.

"He was off the charts in terms of suggestibility," Bergenn recalls. "The authorities convinced him he had done it... so when he denied it, it registered" as a lie on the polygraph.

The police, carefully questioned by Bergenn on his motion to suppress, denied putting any pressure on the defendant. On the contrary, they said, he was very compliant and deferential. The interrogation was easy as pie.

That's when Bergenn called his expert witness, a well-known psychiatrist and expert on hypnosis [Dr. Herbert Spiegel] who had worked on the Peter Reilly case, in which the murder confession of a suggestible Falls Village teenager was eventually thrown out. The psychiatrist testified that Bergenn's client was so suggestible that he was persuaded he must have done what police said he did.

According to Greenspan, "One does not have to be mentally retarded to succumb to the ploys and deceptions used in interrogation sessions."

But courts are reluctant to dismiss confessions, attorney Williams notes. He is asking the state Supreme Court to consider Lapointe's suggestibility in determining his confession to be involuntary, but he acknowledges a paucity of case law supporting that position.

Criminal-defense lawyer Hugh F. Keefe, a partner in New Haven's Lynch, Traub, Keefe and Errante, ticks off a list of categories of cases where people are unduly influenced by police: young people, naive people, submissive people and people raised in cultures where you "agree almost automatically with people in authority."

"The essential test is whether [a confession or the waiver of rights] is knowingly and intelligently made," he says. "It's the trier's call."

The problem, Keefe says, is getting a judge who will not automatically conclude a statement is knowingly and voluntarily made if the defendant meets basic criteria — "an IQ of over 100, an eighth-grade education, speaks English.... It's hard to resist that," Keefe says. "You have to educate the judge on your particular client."

Courts also tend to look not so much at the particularities of the defendant, Bergenn says, as at the methods used by police: "If there are no proverbial rubber hoses, it's not suppressible."

One possible solution, Bergenn says, might be to "establish by a preponderance of evidence that it is not really a freely spoken expression of independent thinking." The confession might not be suppressed, he says, but you could impeach it through the countervailing evidence.

JUDGMENT CALLS

If mental ability, at least as it's measured now, is not an accurate gauge of whether confessions are intelligently and freely given, how are police to tell whether their suspect is confessing because he actually did the crime or because he wants to please them?

Connery says police should adopt the system he says is used in Great Britain. "If there's any indication whatsoever that the suspect has any mental limitations," he says, police should "get in some kind of expert to do testing." Someone familiar with mental retardation should sit in on the police interview, he says.

Connery adds that it's mostly a matter of common sense. "Talk to Lapointe for five minutes and you know he is a limited person," Connery says. "He can't carry on a conversation with any subtleties or complexities."

Keefe says that's too much to ask of police. "You can't expect police, except in the most obvious cases... to be psychologists," he says. "They have a job to do. That's a question for a judge."

Bergenn agrees. "We can't get some cops past racism and sexual stereotyping," he says. "Now you're asking them where someone fits on a social intelligence scale?"

George H. Moore, a former lieutenant colonel in the State Police, doesn't think much of the idea, either.

To measure intelligence accurately, Moore says, "you're talking about somebody with three letters after their name. There aren't too many of those people carrying badges in their back pocket."

As for questions of social intelligence and practical skills, say Moore, a 29-year veteran of the State Police, "That's what defense attorneys are for."

Moore, who retired from the State Police this year, was invited by Connery to take part in a Sept. 16 forum in Hartford on the Lapointe case and others like it. Other scheduled participants were Greenspan, Connery, Peter Reilly, and Pulitzer Prize-winning playwright Arthur Miller, whose efforts helped free Reilly nearly two decades ago. Moore was to speak about the police perspective on the issue of false confessions and videotaping.

A LITTLE BIT OF PLASTIC COULD PROTECT A LOT OF RIGHTS

By PAUL FRISMAN

The Manchester Police Department violated Richard Lapointe's right to due process under the state constitution by failing to record his nine-hour interrogation, says New Haven attorney John R. Williams, who is representing Lapointe on appeal of his murder conviction.

Williams acknowledges that this is a case of first impression, and that the U.S. Supreme Court has not ruled on the issue.

But Williams, of The Law Offices of John R. Williams, argues in his appellate brief that the courts "will always be faced with vexing questions of credibility when police and defendant give contrary accounts of what took place.... In the absence of an electronic record... this Court cannot know, and will never know, whether the defendant was deprived of a fundamental right."

Lapointe was convicted in 1992 after confessing to the murder of his wife's grandmother. On appeal to the Connecticut Supreme Court, he contends that police took advantage of his mental disabilities, manipulating him into making a false confession.

Taping interrogations "is an inexpensive and virtually foolproof method of resolving these credibility issues, offering protection both to those wrongfully accused and to police departments and officers accused of wrongdoing or deception," Williams writes. He cites a 1985 case in which the Alaska Supreme Court required such recordings where feasible. Minnesota also requires taping of police interrogations.

Williams calls upon the state Supreme Court to require taping at least in cases involving possible sentences of death or life imprisonment.

"It's impossible to think of a legitimate reason for not using that little bit of plastic," Williams says in an interview. By reviewing the tape, he says, "the court can say, 'He's disabled, but they [the police] did not overreach,' or, 'Oh, man, this is ridiculous.'"

In Lapointe's case, author and defense supporter Donald Connery says, "I'm convinced a tape would have revealed such a degree of psychological coercion that the confession, so-called, would be seen as utterly invalid.... It's lunatic to think that the state spends hundreds of thousands of dollars for several months of a suppression hearing [which is] totally unnecessary given the fact that someone's invented a recording machine."

The National Institute of Justice found that in 1990, one-sixth of all police and sheriffs' departments — including a third of all departments serving populations of 50,000 or more — videotaped at least some confessions and interrogations.

But in Connecticut, "you won't see it happen" voluntarily, says James W. Bergenn, a defense attorney at Shipman & Goodwin in Hartford. At best, he says, police will tape the actual confession after they have spent hours interrogating a suspect. "There will be real strong resistance," he says, if you "expect them to run a tape from the beginning."

Says criminal-defense specialist Hugh F. Keefe, of New Haven's Lynch, Traub, Keefe and Errante, "It's not a coincidence you don't see many [tapes]. Cops know the downside. You have to be crispy clean. The usual shenanigans that go on — veiled threats, promises that can't be kept — aren't going to fly well at a suppression hearing."

George H. Moore, a retired State Police lieutenant colonel, says that although he believes taping would be "very advantageous," there are many times when it wouldn't be practical, such as when interrogations take place at a crime scene or at somebody's place of work.

"I think it's a great idea, but to require it under all circumstances creates more problems than it solves," he says.

In high-profile cases, Moore thinks police would not object to taping. In those cases, he says, "I'm going to want to do it on my turf. In that case there's no reason it shouldn't be taped."

Taping would benefit both sides, says Brian Kornbrath, assistant clinical professor at the University of Connecticut School of Law's criminal clinic. Police would be able to show confessions made without duress or an accused saying unequivocally he wants to waive his rights. "Absent that, you have the Lapointe case: a swearing match," he says.

Journal Inquirer, Manchester, Connecticut, October 9, 1995

PROSECUTORS DUCK FAIR QUESTIONS ON LAPOINTE AND FALSE CONFESSIONS

By CHRIS POWELL, Managing Editor

At a conference in Hartford the other day sponsored by The Friends of Richard Lapointe, University of California sociology professor Richard Ofshe said criminal investigation produces true and false confessions and that everyone can tell them apart.

But if everyone really could, Lapointe never would have been convicted in 1992 of murdering his wife's grandmother in Manchester five years earlier. And Connecticut never would have heard of another of Lapointe's friends, Peter Reilly, whose conviction for the murder of his mother in Canaan in 1973, a conviction based entirely on a false confession, became the most infamous miscarriage of justice in Connecticut history.

The conference was called "Convicting the Innocent." Its policy goal — as articulated powerfully by Ofshe, Reilly, and the playwright Arthur Miller of Roxbury, who helped get Reilly's conviction overturned almost 20 years ago — was that Connecticut should join Alaska and Minnesota in requiring that, whenever it is practical, confessions in murder cases be recorded rather than merely summarized by police interrogators. The Lapointe case, in which a brain-damaged and suggestible little man signed three highly questionable confessions during a 9½-hour interrogation that was not recorded, makes a compelling argument for such policy.

But the case of Reilly, whose eight-hour interrogation in 1973 *was* recorded, indicates the much larger problem: the lack of recognition of the whole phenomenon of false confession. Without that recognition, no reform is likely to do much good.

Reilly's statements during interrogation resemble the three written confessions obtained from Lapointe by two Manchester police detectives who, despite otherwise elaborate preparations more than two years after the murder they were investigating, somehow couldn't be bothered to set up a tape recorder.

Indeed, there is a pattern to false confessions in murder cases, a pattern of coercion of the vulnerable: The subject at first denies the crime but eventually is worn down into doubting himself and is persuaded that maybe he just doesn't remember or blacked out, and then, tiring, begins acknowledging whatever scenario his interrogators present him, even while failing to produce any original information about the crime and continuing to suggest that he really doesn't believe what he is being led to say. Allowed to recover from the ordeal of interrogation, he repudiates his confession.

Whereupon judges and juries still conclude that no innocent person would ever confess to something so awful — even when a recorded confession like Reilly's shows that the subject is in an exhausted daze and is giving his interrogators no more than what they already have given him.

At the conference in Hartford, Ofshe cited a case from Arizona to predict that 60 percent of the population would confess falsely to murder if forced through a long interrogation. In the Arizona case, a man in a mental hospital came forward to confess to a mass murder, was pressed to identify accomplices, and gave the names of five other people, three of whom confessed during interrogation. But in fact *none of them* had anything to do with the crime, which soon enough was traced to two others, from whom the murder weapon and property stolen from the victims were recovered. And even then, the real culprits were offered leniency if they would implicate any of the five falsely accused people and thereby spare the police the embarrassment of having to admit a mistake. That scheme collapsed.

Connecticut at least should know better than this now because of the Reilly case, in which a conviction based entirely on a repudiated confession was reversed when it was disclosed that the prosecutor had concealed evidence exonerating Reilly and when new evidence strongly implicated others.

Unfortunately, the Lapointe case, in which the only evidence is also a repudiated confession, was complicated by the defendant's physical and mental handicaps, the result of a congenital brain malformation for which he has had surgery many times. While he tests in the low-normal range for ordinary intelligence, he is awkward socially and generally simpleminded. While he has seemed harmless in all other respects, few would consider him normal — which probably only helped the jury to convict him. Indeed, if a jury could convict an otherwise normal teenager like Reilly on the basis of a recorded confession he himself plainly didn't believe even as he was making it, a jury might have convicted Lapointe even if his interrogation had been recorded too.

But maybe not; or maybe Superior Court Judge David M. Barry then might have excluded the confession. For while Reilly was only coaxed and manipulated during his interrogation, there is reason to believe that the detectives who interrogated Lapointe bullied and threatened him and, because of his strangeness, arbitrarily seized on him as the prime suspect two years after the crime and decided to try to break him. If the interrogation really did go that way, as the varying degrees of his written confessions suggest, a recording might have put them in a much different light.

After all, while the Manchester detectives, if they are to be believed, could not be bothered to prepare even the simplest recording device for their long interrogation of Lapointe, they simultaneously were not just tape-recording but tape-recording surreptitiously an interview with his wife at their home, using a hidden microphone and radio transmitter, and the recording was disclosed only by accident.

The better to intimidate Lapointe, the detectives also had prepared the police station and interrogation room with elaborate displays showing false evidence against him.

The detectives must have spent days preparing to snare Lapointe; but if they are to be believed, they decided not to use a tape recorder during his interrogation, even as they took so much trouble to tape-record his wife.

The recording of the interrogation of Lapointe's wife, who suffers from cerebral palsy, shows that the police more or less threatened her with the loss of her son if she didn't incriminate her husband. So it is not hard to imagine that detectives who could surreptitiously tape-record one interrogation and then conceal it could tape-record another one and then conceal or destroy a recording that threatened to impugn a confession they had coerced.

As the Lapointe case moves on appeal to the state Supreme Court, with the legal issue being the admissibility of his confession, his friends, a coalition of the heroes of the Reilly case and advocates for the mentally handicapped, have persuaded the prominent New Haven civil-rights lawyer John Williams to take over the defense from the public defender's office, and they are appealing to public opinion as well.

The conference on false confessions was part of that effort. They also expect to get Lapointe profiled on the CBS network program *60 Minutes*, which most of the country of course would accept as proof of his innocence. And they are hurling challenges at prosecutors, including Chief State's Attorney John Bailey.

While their suggestions that the authorities want to convict an innocent man are hyperbolic, it is good that the struggle is becoming more equal. While prosecutors seem resentful of what Hartford State's Attorney James Thomas dismisses as a *"cause célèbre,"* they generally could use a little more accountability, and there are important questions here in which they should be taking an interest, particularly in regard to the tactics of the Manchester detectives, which the prosecutors continue to ratify.

What do the prosecutors think of the failure of the detectives to tape-record the crucial interrogation when they easily could have recorded it and even as they were recording a less important statement? What does this say about the credibility and integrity of the government's side here? In the age of Mark Fuhrman, would the prosecutors really deny the possibility of improper conduct by police officers? In the age of Peter Reilly, would the prosecutors really deny the possibility of misconduct by one of their own? Would the prosecutors and police deny the phenomenon of false confessions?

To dismiss the Lapointe case as a *"cause célèbre"* is no answer to these questions.

The phenomenon of false confession is real, and it will be a tragic flaw of Connecticut's prosecutors as well as its judges and juries if it is not recognized. For false confessions are too easy to get, and no unrecorded confession that is repudiated and that fails to produce original evidence of the crime should be worth anything. The risk of convicting the innocent is too high.

PART IV

FREEDOM FOR JOHNNY LEE WILSON AND ROLANDO CRUZ;

THE FIGHT FOR RICHARD LAPOINTE GOES ON

Two Injustices
Suddenly Corrected

The press accounts you have just read — the best of many — appeared just days before and days after the September 16 symposium on wrongful convictions.

This surge of attention to the Lapointe case and the concerns it raises was a heady experience for the citizens who had labored long and hard in obscurity to arouse interest in a simple dishwasher whom they proclaimed to be innocent.

Lapointe had suddenly become a national story. Even *60 Minutes* had appeared at the forum to film the event for a report on Connecticut's latest wrong-man scandal.

In truth, however, The Friends of Richard Lapointe would have preferred an awakening of the conscience of the chief state's attorney and speedy efforts to correct the wrong — but this was not to be.

Every effort to get John Bailey and his prosecutors to reconsider their infallibility had drawn a blank. Judging by complaints that appeared in the press, their attitude was this: the accused had every opportunity to put on a defense, a judge had allowed the confession, a jury had found him guilty, the appeal process was now available, so why were these people bothering us?

The idea of a forum had grown out of frustration. Something daring had to be done. But $12,000 or so would have to be raised to put it on, and then would anyone come? Would anyone care?

As things turned out, raising the money, organizing the event, and making it known in just two months was an exhausting high-wire act — but the timing was perfect.

The O.J. Simpson spectacle had shaken public confidence in the justice system. Law enforcement scandals around the nation had revealed mistreatment of minorities and the use of perjured testimony and planted evidence to win convictions. Even the most ardent proponents of law and order now knew what insiders had always known: that the system is fundamentally unfair; that there is one kind of justice for the rich and powerful, another for the poor and powerless.

For The Friends of Richard, simply planning the forum had brought a rush of fresh talent to the organizing sessions at the Burger King and at the Arc office. One stroke of good fortune was the arrival of Marge Cunningham, the founder of one of Connecticut's major court-reporting firms. Her outrage about the Lapointe conviction was such that she offered the full, free services of her company for recording and filming the forum in its entirety.

With every word instantly captured on computer disks, the creation and early publication of this book became possible.

The citizens were feeling lucky. They could not tell Richard Lapointe that any of this activity guaranteed the overturning of his conviction or an early release from prison — the struggle might have to go on for years — but they *could* say that the world was watching.

And then, as if to prove that the Force was with them, two stunning reports came from the Midwest just as this book was being prepared for publication.

First was the news that Johnny Lee Wilson had been set free by the governor of Missouri.

Key members of the Lapointe group had been monitoring developments in that case for years. Robert Perske had written about it in *Unequal Justice?* He and Donald Connery had provided data about confessions and mental retardation for the governor's legal counsel to use as he studied the facts of the wrongful conviction. Johnny Lee's story had been a highlight of the forum.

When the decision to free Wilson was announced, there was nothing mealy-mouthed about it. Here was a straightforward admission by a state's chief executive that an innocent youth had been imprisoned for most of a decade.

This good news was followed soon afterward by word of the release of another innocent young man who had been imprisoned just as carelessly as Lapointe and Wilson. He was Rolando Cruz, convicted of a child's murder in Illinois and sentenced to death in 1985. His was a case that rested not on evidence but on claims made by others: two policemen who said he had told them about a "vision" of the killing, and jailhouse informants who said he had admitted his guilt to them.

So, as we go to press, it is a privilege to conclude this volume in an unexpected way by providing the details of two cases of corrected injustice that can only give heart to those who fight for Richard Lapointe.

STATEMENT BY GOVERNOR MEL CARNAHAN RE: JOHNNY LEE WILSON

Office of the Governor
State of Missouri
Jefferson City, Missouri

As a result of an intense investigation conducted by my office, I have decided to issue a pardon to Johnny Lee Wilson because it is clear he did not commit the crime for which he has been incarcerated.

As governor, one of my most important responsibilities is to protect our citizens from crime.

As you know, I pushed for one of the toughest sentencing laws in the nation, requiring dangerous offenders to serve at least 85 percent of their sentences behind bars — far more than they were serving before this important new law was passed.

I fought for tough new tools for prosecutors, to make it easier to convict child molesters and rapists.

I worked to overhaul our juvenile criminal code so that juvenile criminals would be held accountable for their crimes.

I have worked to put more law enforcement officers on the street, to establish a violent crime support unit, and to implement new, more extensive training requirements for law enforcement officers.

And I have greatly expanded the number of maximum security prison spaces so that dangerous criminals would not be released on the streets prematurely... before they have served their sentences.

My administration has been able to accomplish all of these actions to fight crime because of the power to lead which our forefathers entrusted to the governor.

However, just as I have a responsibility to Missourians to see that criminals are placed behind bars, I also have a responsibility to see that an innocent person is not punished for a crime he did not commit.

It is common for convicted criminals to make claims of innocence. In almost all of these cases, the claims of innocence are false. However, in this case, it is clear that Johnny Lee Wilson's claim is true.

To meet my responsibilities under the Constitution, this office has conducted an exhaustive investigation into the facts of this case. We have spent literally hundreds of hours re-examining the evidence in this case. We have reviewed all the transcripts and re-interviewed the key witnesses including the prosecutor and law enforcement officials involved in this case.

This investigation was conducted by my chief legal counsel, Joe Bednar, a former Jackson County prosecutor who has significant experience in prosecuting homicides and other violent crimes.

From this investigation, it is clear that Johnny Lee Wilson's confession is false and inaccurate. Furthermore, there is no evidence to corroborate or substantiate it. Quite to the contrary, there is significant evidence to indicate that it is false.

It is evident that the only facts this mentally retarded man knew about this hideous crime were the facts given to him by investigators who felt pressure to solve the case quickly. And virtually all the information Wilson himself tried to offer about the crime — in response to the investigators' questions — was inaccurate and inconsistent with the known facts.

In fact, the original motivation for Wilson's arrest has been removed. The person who originally accused Wilson of committing the crime has recanted his accusation and now admits that the statement he made to police was untrue.

As long as I am governor, we will strive to lock away violent criminals so they won't be in our schools and won't be in our neighborhoods.

But in the case of Johnny Lee Wilson, we have locked up an innocent, retarded man who is not guilty of the crime of which he was accused.

Therefore, as governor of the State of Missouri, I am issuing a pardon to Johnny Lee Wilson.

In addition to the recommendation from my Chief Counsel, the Probation and Parole Board has also recommended that I take this action.

My office will continue to work closely with law enforcement officials to see that the person who did commit this horrible crime is found, prosecuted, and punished.

INNOCENT, AND FREE AT LAST

A Missouri Case Shows How the Retarded Get Railroaded in Court

When the word came, Johnny Lee Wilson, Inmate No. 160230 in Cellblock 5A at the Jefferson City Correctional Center, was in the 10th year of a life sentence without parole for a murder he knew he had not committed. Just moments before, Missouri Gov. Mel Carnahan had signed a pardon. Wilson was disbelieving when, at the maximum security prison seven blocks from the governor's office, guards handed him a brown envelope with the $7.31 from his inmate account. For the first time in his adult life, he was a free man.

Wilson's case has illuminated a little-known problem that bedevils the nation's legal system: the tendency of mildly retarded defendants to make false confessions. Police in Wilson's tiny Ozark town suspected him in the 1986 death of family friend Pauline Martz, 79, and during a four-hour interrogation Wilson seemed to confess. But last Friday, Governor Carnahan said a yearlong review found that Wilson, now 30, had simply given police answers he thought would get him out of trouble. "We have locked up an innocent retarded man who is not guilty," Carnahan said. A 1994 investigation by *U.S. News* helped spur the review that led to last week's pardon.

Easily confused, scared and eager to please, people with retardation often are quick to "confess" to crimes they did not commit. Police and defense lawyers are rarely trained to spot mild retardation or the behavior that can produce false confessions. "There are Johnny Wilsons in every state in the country," says Bob Perske, an advocate who tracks such cases.

U.S. News surveyed more than two dozen cases pointed out as troubling by experts in retardation and criminal justice and found patterns of behavior that help explain why suspects with retardation and brain damage can be falsely accused and convicted.

They hide their limitations. To be labeled retarded is so stigmatizing that retarded people go to great lengths to "pass" for normal. The easiest way to hide an inability to understand, says University of New Mexico special education Prof. Ruth Luckasson, is to rely on "a person who's smarter," particularly an authority figure like a parent or police officer. A frightened Wilson thought he could trust police, and by following their leading questions and suggestions, he gave details of the murder from the color of the victim's blouse to how she was bound with duct tape.

They lack understanding. Manchester, Conn., police had the "goods" on Richard Lapointe. They put it on a dozen charts on the station walls for the confused man with congenital brain damage to see when he was questioned about the rape and murder of his wife's grandmother. One listed evidence — "Fingerprints," "DNA Test," "Pubic Hair," with big red checks next to each. It was all phony, a trick to coax a confession. Someone else might have spotted the nonsense. After all, detectives "Friday" and "Gannon" from television's *Dragnet* were named on the sham "Homicide Task Force." But after nine hours of interrogation, Lapointe offered a confession of sorts: "If the evidence shows that I was there, and that I killed her, then I killed her, but I don't remember being there."

A Connecticut jury convicted him, despite the lack of eyewitnesses and solid physical evidence, and in spite of police admissions that they used trickery to get his confession. Police insist they got the right man, but last month 225 people, including playwright Arthur Miller, gathered in Hartford to demand a reconsideration of the case. They noted parallels with cases such as that of David Vasquez of Virginia, who confessed to murdering a woman in her home after police falsely claimed that witnesses and fingerprints tied him to the crime scene. Vasquez was pardoned in 1989 after spending five years in confinement.

The criminal justice system can be a dizzying place for defendants with limited intelligence. Lapointe says he confessed so police would let him use the bathroom; Wilson says he thought he would be allowed to go home. When Chuck Mathenia's death sentence was temporarily stayed in 1993, the retarded man did not understand that his life had been saved: he was angry to lose the free canteen privileges given to inmates on Missouri's Death Row.

Retarded people who confess to crimes seldom win back their freedom unless other suspects come forth. Wilson would have been forgotten if Chris Brownfield, a career criminal, had not confessed and added telling details of the murder. Similarly, after spending nine years behind bars, John Purvis of Florida was freed when a hit man who had become deeply religious admitted that he had been hired by the victim's former husband to kill her. Gerald Delay spent seven months in a Kansas jail before a conscience-stricken witness came forward with testimony that freed him. Earl Washington was removed from Death Row after nearly 10 years, but only after a DNA test showed he was not guilty, despite his confession to a rape in Virginia. [He is still imprisoned.]

Death Row cases cause the most concern. Although retarded people make up 2 to 3 percent of the prison population — about the same as their numbers in the general population — they have accounted for almost 13 percent of executions, reports Amnesty International.

Death penalty foes have jumped on questionable cases to argue against capital punishment. Great Britain banned executions in 1964 after Timothy Evans, a retarded man who was hanged for murdering his wife and child, was posthumously found innocent. The U.S. Supreme Court ruled 5-4 in 1989 that it is not unconstitutional to execute retarded people. Nevertheless, 10 states have banned such executions since 1988.

Opposition to laws barring execution has come from a surprising source: some retarded people themselves. In Texas and California, people with developmental disabilities fought and defeated such bans, arguing that seeking exceptions from the law would contradict their demands to be mainstreamed into society. "If we are to have rights, we must have responsibilities," says Kevin Tracy of Texas Advocates.

Some retarded defendants, indeed, are guilty, such as Sylvester Adams, who was convicted of murder and executed recently in South Carolina. (A quirk in Washington, D.C., law allowed a retarded man who killed his roommate to go free last week, after he was found incompetent to stand trial but ineligible for psychiatric commitment.) But most advocates question whether any people with retardation can adequately take part in their own defense, a condition that the Constitution says is necessary in order to receive a fair trial.

The Nightmare Ends for Rolando Cruz

Illinois Man, On Death Row for 11 Years, Set Free After Retrial

On November 4, 1995, the long ordeal of Rolando Cruz was finally over. A judge, angered by admissions of police perjury, brought "a stunning end," as the Chicago *Tribune* reported, "to a case that has confounded defense lawyers and exhausted prosecutors, a case that exposed the frailties and imperfections of American justice."

What follows are the highlights of the Cruz story as told in earlier media reports and summarized by the *Tribune*, *The New York Times*, and the Associated Press on the first day of his freedom.

A Refusal to Admit Error

"Growing up poor and Latino in Aurora, Illinois," wrote Salim Muwakkil in the April 4, 1994 issue of *In These Times*, "Rolando Cruz never had an easy life. But just before he turned 20, things got considerably worse: he was charged with kidnapping, raping and murdering 10-year-old Jeanine Nicarico from nearby Naperville. And despite a glaring lack of evidence linking him to the crime and a convicted killer's confession of guilt in the girl's murder, Cruz now sits on Death Row.

"The 1983 crime traumatized the region, a Republican stronghold noted primarily for its high level of suburban amenities. After more than a year without a credible suspect, public pressure provoked the DuPage County Sheriff's Department to charge Cruz and a friend named Alejandro Hernandez with Nicarico's abduction, rape and murder. The two were tried and convicted in February 1985 despite the lack of direct evidence linking them to the crime.

"In fact, the only incriminating data was a 'vision' Cruz was said to have had of the Nicarico murder that closely conformed in its details to the actual crime. This story was first recounted by two sheriff's detectives during the course of the trial, and although it was never recorded or corroborated, the vision story was the evidence most responsible for Cruz's first conviction.

"Several months later, a suspect who had been arrested in the abduction, rape and murder of a seven-year-old girl from LaSalle County, Illinois, confessed to that slaying and volunteered information about two others: a woman in Kane County, Illinois, named Donna Schnorr — *and Jeanine Nicarico*. The suspect, Brian Dugan, said he acted alone and offered to provide testimony that would exonerate Cruz and Hernandez, if he could plea-bargain for a life sentence without possibility of parole instead of a death sentence.

"Both Kane and LaSalle Counties accepted Dugan's confession for the crimes in their respective areas, but DuPage officials refused. After all, they had already solved the county's most celebrated murder mystery, and the two men sitting on Death Row were their trophies."

CITIZEN SUPPORT

And so began a roller-coaster ride through the legal system for Cruz and Hernandez. The prosecutors were relentless despite a wealth of evidence — including the results of DNA tests — that Brian Dugan was the murderer. A succession of judgments in many courts over 12 years led to an 80-year prison sentence for Hernandez, later reversed (he finally was set free in late 1995), and what seemed to be a permanent place on Death Row for Cruz.

Because an execution is so final, it was Cruz who became the primary object of attention by concerned citizens who recognized the enormity of the injustice. Hernandez, however, found a famous defender: Scott Turow, the former federal prosecutor and best-selling novelist.

In February 1994, funds collected by the Northwestern University Legal Clinic helped pay for "A Forum on Wrongful Convictions" that was hosted by an impressive array of individuals and organizations, including Amnesty International, the Cook County Bar Association, and the MacArthur Justice Center.

The featured speakers were Rubin "Hurricane" Carter, the former middleweight contender who had served 19 years in prison for crimes he did not commit, and Randall Adams, subject of the film *The Thin Blue Line*, who was framed for the murder of a Texas police officer and spent 11 years on Death Row before he was exonerated and released, largely because of public reaction to the film.

OFFICERS PROTEST

Public support for Cruz was greatly enhanced by the astonishing fact that one law enforcement officer after another broke ranks to say, in effect, that the prosecutors were railroading Rolando Cruz. They included the former director of the Illinois State Police whose agency investigated the case; one of the DuPage County detectives who led the original murder investigation; the former chief of the DuPage County Crime Laboratory who resigned in protest over the prosecutors' illegal suppression of evidence that refuted the claims of Cruz's guilt; the former chief of police of Naperville, where the crime occurred; and the former state's attorney of Kane County, who said that public recognition of the official misconduct in the case "will do to prosecutors what the Rodney King beating tapes have done to the police."

Typically, however, the continuing exposure of the miscarriage of justice did little to slow the career of the state's attorney who was primarily reponsible for the repeated prosecutions. James Ryan has moved on to become the elected attorney general of Illinois. He is considered a strong Republican contender for the governorship.

Rolando Cruz's most prominent attorney, Northwestern University law professor Lawrence Marshall, said that "One of the greatest satisfactions of publicizing the injustices in this case is the fact that we caught one of the chinks in the system. Who would have thought there would be so much fuss over these two poor Latino kids from Aurora?"

FAILURE TO RECORD

All the fuss led to a bench trial in the DuPage County District Court in late October 1995. Once again, the two cops testified that Cruz had told them of a dream he had had of seeing a young girl's body.

This time, however, one of their supervisors admitted during questioning that he had lied earlier when he confirmed the officers' story. In fact, he had been in Florida at the time he was supposed to have spoken with them about Cruz's "vision."

Did the cops lie as well? According to the *Tribune*, the judge seemed to think so. He wondered why they had not bothered to provide any kind of record of what the suspect said, if indeed he said anything.

"Tape-recorded statements," he observed in his acquittal ruling, "preserve all the evidence. The court likes... anything that can be verified... things I can see and touch and feel."

Said the Chicago *Tribune*:

"With criticism of the prosecutors dripping from his voice, DuPage Circuit Judge Ronald Mehling set Cruz free, and a man who had spent years on Death Row was hustled out of the courthouse to freedom. He said he wanted a rib dinner."

Afterword

What have we learned? What do we want? What's next?

This summing-up will tell you — after we answer two more obvious questions:

Why do we bother? Why do we care?

After all, with the exception of three faithful relatives, none of The Friends of Richard Lapointe knew him before his trial. We were unaware of his existence unless we had glanced at the all-too-routine stories in the local papers about a murder and the arrest of a man who had confessed to the crime.

We certainly knew nothing of him during the nearly three years he waited in prison — virtually without visitors — for a chance to be judged by a jury of his peers.

This was no O.J. Simpson case. The victim was not prominent or glamorous; the accused was not rich, famous or influential. He was one of society's invisibles: one of the millions who drive the trucks, fix the wires, dig the ditches, wash the dishes, and make the nation work.

Those of us who first noticed the injustice had no idea that it could become a nationally known wrong-man case. We had no conception that it might, just possibly, set off a chain reaction of reforms in America's deeply flawed justice system.

We simply felt that it was unfair and indecent to treat a fellow human being this way, especially one whose mental and physical limitations were so obvious and so easily exploited.

As a nation, Americans preach to others about human rights, yet here was a matter of human rights on our own doorstep. Lure an innocent man from his home *on Independence Day*, force a false confession, put him behind bars, and then demand that he be put to death — can it get any worse than that in the land of the free and the home of the brave?

When schoolyard bullies pounce on a blameless youngster who is the one least able to defend himself, you can either look away or try to stop it.

When the state — not for the first time — mindlessly demolishes a man and his family to close its files on an unsolved homicide, you can either remain silent or shout for all the world to hear.

In truth, however, we spent little time in our Burger King skull sessions discussing why each of us was motivated to come to Lapointe's assistance. What Arthur Miller told an interviewer was good enough for us all (and he said it much better): "I feel doubly obligated to speak when I think silence would mean some kind of complicity on my part."

What we *did* talk about ceaselessly was the American injustice system — as we sometimes thought of it.

This was not a pleasant thought. We preferred to believe in the people who serve as our protectors. A number of us had friends and relatives who were police officers, prosecutors, judges, and prison guards. Indeed, several of us had been or would soon be cops and guards. In a crime-ridden nation, we were just as anxious as everyone else to identify and punish the guilty.

We had no sympathy for anyone who savagely takes a life. Mrs. Martin and her family deserved to have true justice done. Why let an innocent man rot in prison while a murderer, in Miller's words, enjoys his "passport to freedom"?

So we pooled our knowledge, taught each other, and called in experts to tell us more. Some of us came with long experience in the law, in mental retardation and learning disabilities, and in psychology and psychiatry. Several of us, as writers, were deeply informed about other cases of wrongful conviction.

We learned that miscarriages of justice occur far, far more often than the public knows or the system admits. Because the vast majority of those who are arrested, prosecuted and convicted *are* guilty, or at least have been engaged in some kind of wrongdoing, it has been all too easy to ignore the obvious and the inevitable: that wholly innocent persons will be consumed in an imperfect process directed by imperfect people.

How many? Far more, for sure, than the limited and conservative calculations of the experts. Most studies have been restricted to capital or potentially capital crimes and established instances of wrongful convictions. But the hundreds of reported examples of proven innocence say nothing about the unknown thousands of men and women who have been erroneously imprisoned or even executed for major crimes over the years.

They were doomed from the first accusation. Unlike Johnny Lee Wilson, Rolando Cruz, and others who have been dramatically rescued, they were denied the benefit of dedicated attorneys, concerned citizens, or press exposures of perjured testimony or concealed evidence. The true rapists and murderers did not step forward to claim responsibility.

"What is striking" about cases with happy endings, writes Gisli Gudjonsson, a London-based expert on American and British miscarriages of justice, "is that so many of the defendants were proven innocent by sheer luck and good fortune."

As for individuals charged with lesser crimes, C. Ronald Huff and Arye Rattner, the authors of a forthcoming book, *Convicted But Innocent: Ten Years of Research*, use 1990 statistics to conservatively estimate that, of some 2 million convictions, more than 10,000 persons are wrongfully imprisoned or otherwise punished in America each year.

In an interview on the CBS Evening News just days before this book went to press, Jim McCloskey of Centurion Ministries said that "There are thousands and thousands of completely innocent people buried in prison for horrendous crimes done by others."

Why so many wrongful convictions? The answers already provided in these pages coincide with numerous studies that put faulty eyewitness testimony, witness perjury, police mistakes, and coerced confessions high among the reasons for miscarriages of justice.

A *Christian Science Monitor* survey in 1995 cited public pressure to solve crimes, police eagerness to pin the crime on the most convenient suspect, suppression of evidence, reliance on jailhouse informants, spurious "scientific" evidence, and biased judges as common factors that imprison the innocent instead of the guilty.

Arresting Richard Lapointe for Bernice Martin's murder, for example, "gives every appearance of being the type of matter in which the police over-reacted [to public demands that they solve the crime]... It is a sad fact that this type of arrest goes on every day, albeit not on such a grand or tragic scale."

These are the words of a retired Connecticut police officer, fourteen years on the force, who closely examined the Martin murder and Lapointe prosecution in 1994-95 for a law school thesis on police attitudes and practice. Christine J.P. Myers — assisted by her husband, a veteran homicide and arson investigator who is now a private detective — tells of the "deep sense of paranoia among police" and how the worst cops can behave "in devastating ways." She speaks of the insufficient training of police recruits about the constitutional foundations of laws protecting suspects.

She writes: "I contend that the Manchester police did not have probable cause to arrest Richard Lapointe up until the point when he gave his confessions." They "bombarded" him with accusatorial statements in an "inherently coercive" incommunicado interrogation. Certain details of his so-called admissions are convincing only if one "suspends all reason."

Cases like *Lapointe*, *Reilly* and others, Christine Myers says, "illustrate just how easily the mentally retarded or socially challenged can be manipulated by figures of authority, particularly those whom they respect and admire, like the police.... The Manchester police did not have to work very hard to break this suspect. They were dealing with a very needy, vulnerable man locked in the mind of a child. They had won their battle before it even began."

Such police excesses, of course, lead to wrongful convictions only because of the zeal of prosecutors to win cases at no matter what cost to justice. The inclination of the least competent or least principled is to uncritically accept and swiftly validate police conclusions about a crime, however implausible.

Not all prosecutors, to be sure, but the rotten apples seem to be overflowing the barrel — all to the detriment of the true professionals who believe, as did Connecticut's Homer Cummings in the 1924 case of *State vs. Israel*, that "It is just as important for a state's attorney to use the great powers of his office to protect the innocent as to convict the guilty."

The Friends of Richard Lapointe have noticed something extraordinary: that in the very years of their struggle to free one man, the whole nation seems to be going through an orgy of false accusations and reckless prosecutions.

As if it were not enough to rely so excessively on extracting confessions in the familiar realm of law enforcement, all too many police and prosecutors — taking their cues from overzealous psychotherapists and social workers — have ridden roughshod over the civil rights and reputations of thousands of innocent persons as they charge parents and day-care providers with sex crimes against children.

The very real and troubling cases of incest and other forms of child abuse have been diminished by a wave of hysteria about so-called recovered memories and imagined satanic rituals that has engulfed and destroyed families by the thousands.

The tide is turning. The work of the False Memory Syndrome Foundation, revelations in books like *Victims of Memory* and *Making Monsters*, exposés by public television's *Frontline*, investigations by *The Wall Street Journal* and other newspapers, the overturning of convictions in such day-care cases as McMartin, Edonton, Kelly Michaels and Fells Acre — all signal a vast leap in public awareness that should limit the excesses of prosecutors.

But what of false confessions? And what of the continuing abuse of persons with mental disabilities — whether innocent or guilty — as they encounter the criminal justice system? They too need the cleansing impact of aroused public opinion.

As evidenced by this book and the forum that brought it into being, these have been major concerns of the citizens working to free Richard Lapointe. We believe his case is worthy of being *the* case that educates the nation about the reasons why such injustices happen and the things that can be done to stop them.

THE REFORM AGENDA

It is our ambition and our intention to work in Connecticut for certain reforms and then to work with others to get them established in every state.

You have read the book; you know what we are about:

1. **We believe that a confession should be considered worthless if there is no corroborating evidence.**

   Think about the numerous false confession episodes related in these pages. Then consider Washington state's now-famous Paul Ingram case of 1988-89, as told in Lawrence Wright's *Re-*

membering Satan.

Ingram, the supremely suggestible former member of the Thurston County Sheriff's Department, "confessed" to a multitude of horrifying crimes — everything from marathon episodes of incest to murders committed as part of a nationwide satanic conspiracy. Though his statements to a succession of bewildered but relentless interrogators were demonstrably false, with not a shred of evidence confirming his ramblings, he was advised to plead guilty to six counts of third-degree rape and accept a 20-year sentence in a federal prison. He remains there still, aware at last that he is no monster and hopeful that the justice system will also come to its senses.

2. **We believe police everywhere should be required to videotape, in their entirety, interrogations that produce confessions, true or false.**

The common-sense argument for this idea has been made here by many voices. Though the document that most powerfully lays the groundwork for this reform is the huge National Institute of Justice study to which Paul Frisman refers in his article "A Little Bit of Plastic Could Protect A Lot of Rights," Peter Reilly's comment in his forum speech may say it all: "I was appalled that a child could tape-record the President of the United States but a professional police department could fail to record the interrogation of Richard Lapointe."

3. **We believe that persons with mental disabilities should not be left to fend for themselves when confronted by police interrogators. They should have someone to help them appreciate their constitutional rights, understand the questions, and know the consequences of their answers.**

Yes, this would require police interrogators to be on the lookout for signs of intellectual impairment, but so what? They are trained observers. Some suspects are already known in the community to be "slow" or "childlike."

Any good detective should be able to identify even the mildly retarded — including those who try to disguise their limitations by claiming to understand the Miranda warning.

And many a conscientious officer would not object to the kind of solution (to quote from an official document) that has proven effective in Great Britain: the assignment of an "appropriate adult" — often a social worker — "to advise the person being questioned and to observe whether or not the interview is being conducted properly and fairly, and secondly, to facilitate communication with the person being interviewed."

4. **We believe there should be fair and automatic recompense for the wrongly convicted.**

An individual erroneously imprisoned for years should get a substantial payment to make up for his lost income and for the suffering that only the convicted innocent know.

As things stand, the fifty states have different attitudes and rules on this matter. Like Peter Reilly, most of the unjustly convicted get nothing, yet in rare instances, thanks to legislative or legal action, the victim of injustice may be awarded a million dollars or more.

Neither the innocent person released from prison nor those speaking on his behalf (as we will for Richard Lapointe) should have to plead with the governor and the legislators to do the right thing. As in Ohio, there should be a system and a fund in place to provide an appropriate or ample recompense (depending on the number of years of lost liberty and other factors) while avoiding excessive claims on the state's treasury.

The wonder is that something so obviously fair and decent is not common practice everywhere. More than sixty years ago, in *Convicting the Innocent*, Edwin Borchard said that "the least the State can do to vindicate itself and make restitution to the innocent victim is to grant him an indemnity, not as a matter of grace and favor but as a matter of right."

Truth and Justice First

The remedies just outlined are hardly cure-alls, but if widely established, they would at least modify the never-ending plague of erroneous convictions.

What is most required is a dedication to putting truth and justice first. We are still mired in the 1930s when, as Professor Borchard observed, it was "common knowledge that the prosecuting technique in the United States is to regard a conviction as a personal victory calculated to enhance the prestige of the prosecutor."

In the Lapointe case, a zeal for truth and justice would have led to any number of steps to make sure that the crime had been properly solved with the right man, especially after the first alarms were sounded about an apparent injustice.

The most obvious move would have been to ask Dr. Henry Lee to examine the Bernice Martin murder in its entirety (including such crime-scene details as the pair of black driver's gloves, too large for the victim or the accused, that were found on the bed and floor and then totally disregarded once the preferred suspect was brought to trial).

Dr. Lee, who directs Connecticut's magnificently equipped State Police Forensic Science Laboratory, is simply the nation's best known and most respected criminalist. His skills and objectivity have been sought in dozens of baffling homicide cases across the country. He was called to California to examine the murders made famous in the O.J. Simpson case. Yet he has been kept out of the most controversial major-crime event in his own state.

Clearly, the prosecutors dare not ask Dr. Lee to take a look. His conclusions could be embarrassing — as they were to the Virginia authorities when his findings helped save Earl Washington from execution.

Does this mean that they *know* Lapointe is innocent?

Probably not. No doubt they have convinced themselves that they are right. There is such a thing as willful ignorance, and their ignorance of confession phenomena and variations of mental impairments appears to be profound. Moreover, the bureaucratic mindset says that a man is guilty because we say he is guilty and because we have other cases to work on; there are so many of them.

G.K. Chesterton said, "The horrible thing about all legal officials, even the best, about all judges, magistrates, detectives and policemen, is not that they are wicked (some of them are good), not that they are stupid (some of them are quite intelligent), it is simply that they have got used to it."

And no longer care about true justice.

But *we* must not get used to it. Or stop caring.

Easy Guide to Ten Major Topics

Index of Names